JODY THOMAS

Why, Mommy, Why?

DISSOCIATIVE IDENTITY DISORDER

Green Effect Media

BOLINGBROOK, IL

WWW.GREENEFFECTMEDIA.COM

Text and illustrations copyright © 2009 by Jody Thomas

Cover design by Green Effect Media

All rights reserved. Published in the United States by Green Effect Media, Bolingbrook, IL. No portion of this book may be reproduced, in whole or in part, without written permission of the publisher.

Green Effect Media books are available at a special discount when purchased in bulk for educational use. Special editions or book excerpts can also be created to specification. Green Effect Media also publishes its books in a variety of electronic formats.

For more information, contact the publisher at the address below.

Green Effect Media
P.O. Box 1888
Bolingbrook, IL 60440

www.GreenEffectMedia.com

ISBN: 978-0-578-03026-5

Printed in the United States of America.

First Edition: July 2009
10 9 8 7 6 5 4 3 2 1

Acknowledgements

There are many wonderful people who have aided me in my recovery from a difficult and painful childhood. First and foremost are my husband and my son, who stood by me through my long therapy process. Also, mere words are insufficient to thank Dr. Jim and Dr. Norm who guided me through the steps of my joyful recovery. Without them, I never would have achieved a life of joy and peace. I also wish to thank them for their efforts in helping me tell my story.

My medical doctors, Dr. Bruce and his partner, Dr. Helen, deserve special thanks for their gentle care and support, unfailing belief in me, and expertise in coordinating my medical asthma treatment with my psychiatric care.

I also wish to thank my friend, Joyce, who I met in therapy, as she has been both a role model and an inspiration to me during my therapy and remains a close friend today.

All of my new friends who I have met during the past several years have also helped me become who I am today.

I also thank Lynn W. at *Many Voices*, as her newsletter of hope has helped me through some very hard times during my journey.

Author's Note

I have written this book under the pseudonym Jody Thomas for personal anonymity. Some of the names of persons and places have been changed to protect identities, dignity and privacy.

Dedication

This book is dedicated to my husband and to my son, whose unfailing support helped me through this journey. They have stood by me throughout my recovery.

This book is also dedicated to Dr. Jim and to Dr. Norm. Without their expertise, compassion and endless patience, I never would have achieved a life free from pain, and filled with joy.

FORWARD

PART ONE: *DEVELOPING THE CONSTITUTION—LAWS FOR SURVIVAL*

INTRODUCTION
THE CONSTITUTION

PART TWO: *TRAUMA LEADS TO ASTHMA—ASTHMA LEADS TO THERAPY*

PART THREE: *BEGINNING TO REMEMBER*

THE ORIGINAL CONSTITUTION
AMENDMENT I
AMENDMENT II
AMENDMENT III
AMENDMENT IV
AMENDMENT V

PART FOUR: *DISSOCIATION—DISABILITY—HOSPITALIZATIONS*

AMENDMENT VI

PART FIVE: *THE BEGINNING OF A NEW LIFE—BACK TO WORK*

AMENDMENT VII

PART SIX: *MEETING JESSIE*

AMENDMENT VIII
A LETTER TO MOM

CONCLUSION

Why, Mommy, Why?

Forward

There have been many books written about, and by, individuals who endured enormous trauma and abuse as children. The authors describe their courageous efforts in surviving and overcoming the effects of that trauma, inspiring many readers with the promise of hope and change their stories offer.

Some readers may find it easier to put books like these down because their stories seem too painful, or because they hit too close to home. Some readers will focus on the incidents and severity of abuse, what I call the cathartic drama. Other readers may raise questions about how alleged loved ones could have perpetrated such acts while family members were able to simply look the other way.

You will find all of those issues explored here.

What sets Jody's account apart is her ability to articulate in detail the steps toward the restoration of her "Self." Jody describes the process of respecting and integrating her various identities, dispelling negative beliefs about herself and transforming them into positive ones.

Competent psychotherapy and psychiatric management has helped many clients heal from trauma. Jody's account offers unique insight into that therapeutic process from the patient's perspective. Her ability to articulate the methods used in such detail is rare. Rarer still is her unique understanding of what lay at the heart of the healing process.

Jody's book is not just about telling her story to a compassionate reader. It is not about the gory details of abuse, nor is it about the physical effects of trauma. Her account explores the extreme defenses we are capable of developing to survive and how, later, these same defenses begin to work against us. Jody explores complex issues regarding the damage that can be done to a child's self-perception and how the adult that child develops into navigates the outside world.

As a reader, try not to see Jody as different from the rest of us. We may not all have several identities with individual names and personalities, but we all have different parts of ourselves that we must reconcile to become more whole and open to life. We all operate out of belief systems that are compellingly irrational.

The formulas and recipes for recovery that Jody suggests can be applied to each of us. Cognitive behavioral therapy and emotion focused methods, two key techniques Jody describes in her account, can be just as beneficial for everyday conflicted individuals as they are for patients with dissociative disorders.

Likewise, self psychology has extensively mapped the damage to the self that can occur—in many of us to varying degrees—as a result of early messages we receive from our much-needed caregivers, whose love we hope for. Those messages give rise to irrational childhood beliefs about ourselves and the world around us that follow us into adulthood.

Jody details the work required to change her beliefs with amazing precision and creativity. She chooses the language of the Constitution and amendments to The Constitution to express what cognitive behavioral therapists would call schemas. Gradually, she moves from the certainty that she is "bad" and "unlovable" to a balanced perception of her strengths and weaknesses. She moves from being consumed by emotional toxins crippling her body toward breaking free.

As Jody's primary therapist, I appreciate and understand how so many people played crucial roles in her incredible journey. Jody's ability to reach out to others was essential to her healing process. Competent medication management and a collaborative effort with her psychiatrist, Dr. Norm, were essential. Clients need to hear similar positive messages in different ways, from different people.

Therapists reading Jody's account will find numerous examples of therapeutic interventions detailed here. They may see some mistakes I made over the 17 years of Jody's treatment, as the thinking about dissociative disorders has evolved in that time. Feel free to be critical, question, and develop your own ideas.

This story is told entirely from Jody's perspective. She writes in everyday language that will be compelling to any reader. I believe her exploration of the power and importance of how our self-concept evolves, adapts, and changes is universal to all great character development.

Jody is the hero of this story, an abusive childhood the villain, and her therapists, family and friends the supporting cast.

— Dr. Jim
June, 2009

Part One

DEVELOPING THE CONSTITUTION — LAWS FOR SURVIVAL

Why, Mommy, Why?

Introduction

I believe I developed Multiple Personality Disorder, today called Dissociative Identity Disorder, at a very early age—certainly younger than five. This is my story: of abuse and terror, of treatment, of unrelenting physical illness and emotional turmoil and, in the end, of joy and hope and a truly fulfilling, peaceful life.

This story is titled, *Why, Mommy, Why?* because—although many people were involved in the abuse that caused me to develop alter personalities as a means of survival—my mother was the main perpetrator of confusion, horror, and the unimaginable complexities of guilt I had to contend with throughout my childhood. I believe my mother was most likely mentally ill. I know she was put on psychotropic medication by the time I was in high school.

My childhood consisted up growing up in a home that was *silent*, except for my mother's tirades. My parents never spoke to each other, didn't even acknowledge they lived in the same house. My only brother, Matthew, was older than me, and had already moved out by the time I was growing up.

Although this story is filled with memories of abuse—physical, sexual, and emotional—the worst thing of all, and the hardest to deal with in therapy—were all the "messages," the beliefs my mother so firmly ingrained in my mind.

My therapy involved years of meeting my alters—Ronnie, Jenny, Jennifer, The Little One, She, Jeff, Janet, Little Jody and Jessie—and years of sharing their memories. Through it all, my underlying belief was that I was abused because I was bad, and more than that: *all the bad things that happened in the world were my fault*. Bad things happened because I was a bad girl.

There was a pervasive sense of guilt underlying every form of abuse from my mother, which it would take me over 17 years of therapy to effectively combat. All of my crises, my suicidal thoughts, my self-destructive behaviors, my constant desire to run away, were all borne out of this sense of guilt.

When I was six or seven years old, Mother used to lock me out of the house when I came home from school. She wouldn't let me in until I took my clothes off outside and urinated on the backyard lawn. Then, she'd let me in and beat me with a leather strap for behaving like an animal.

That was the type of "guilt contradiction" I had to contend with a daily basis. But her messages weren't confined to things I did or didn't do. When our neighbors' house burnt down, she said the fire started because I didn't behave right that day.

I was to blame for *everything*. By adulthood, that message had been so ingrained that I truly came to believe that everything I heard about on the news was my fault.

From childhood:
Didn't my father sexually abuse me because I was bad?
Didn't my friend Paul die because I killed him when I was five years old?
Didn't I need to be locked in the garage without food or water because I was bad for talking to my friends?
Didn't my mother have eye and heart problems because I didn't listen?
Wasn't our house infested with flies because I was "garbage?"

Into adulthood:
Didn't that car crash happen because I wrote in my journal that I was angry with my mother?
Didn't hundreds of people die in the Oklahoma City Bombing because I had an abortion?

Those are some of the issues and thought processes I had to learn to change in therapy. In this book, you'll meet Dr. Jim and Dr. Norm. It was with their help, in the end, that I finally came to believe I am *not bad*.

Beginning at age five, long before I met them, I developed "Laws" for survival in order to survive my childhood—my own personal "Constitution." You will see how I passed amendments as I grew up and as my situation changed.

Why, Mommy, Why?

The Constitution
Ratified in 1963 – five years old

We, Jody and the sum of all the alters, in order to form a union for survival, provide for a common defense, and promote safety for all, do establish this Constitution for daily living. We will live according to its laws, which is the only way to ensure our survival in a world of abuse and terror.

These laws shall include, but are not limited to:

Never go along with what Mother tells us to do.

Stay as far away from her as possible.

Stay with Dad as much as possible for safety.

Never show any feelings—especially never show that the beatings hurt us in any way.

Allow whichever alter is best suited to the situation to be in control.

The alters must never tell each other what they had to do while in control.

Each alter may decide the best course of action for survival in each situation.

Always rebel in the face of adversity.

Always use dissociation for safety.

AMENDMENT I—1969—11 YEARS OLD

This amendment was proposed and accepted when Dad abandoned Jody at age 11.

We have the right to run away from home as often as the need arises, as there is no longer any safety at home.

We have the right to try to enlist outside help—by attempting to talk to the police, priests, nuns, doctors, social workers, anyone.

Amendment II—1971—13 years old

This amendment was proposed and accepted when two years of trying to get help failed, and we ended up in a state psychiatric hospital.

From this point on, it will no longer be acceptable to reach out to other people, as this only results in further punishment and further reduction of safety.

We must never talk honestly with other people again. We must never have true friendships.

Should a friendship inadvertently arise, we must sabotage it to maintain safety.

Only Jeff will interact with Dad.

We will continue to never show feelings. We will allow Jennifer to have control, since she has no feelings.

We will, from this point forward, live life as a stone statue.

Should any feelings inadvertently arise, we will cut ourselves with scissors or razor blades to eliminate them.

Amendment III—1976—17 years old

This amendment was proposed and accepted following a failed suicide attempt at age seventeen.

As life is intolerable and even suicide does not work, we will, from this point on, live life as an "actress."

We will completely forget the past and live life as though nothing bad has ever happened to us.

We will survive by keenly observing other people and "acting" as a "normal" person based on those observations.

We never will be honest with other people and will avoid friends at all costs.

Amendment IV—1979—20 years old

This amendment was proposed and accepted when Jody got married and received a nursing degree.

We will observe how married people behave and "act" accordingly.

We will function as *one person* in the workplace in order to hide our true identities and to survive.

Amendment V—1981—22 years old

This amendment was proposed and accepted when our son was born.

We amend our decision to never have feelings. We allow *one* feeling: Love Rich unconditionally.

At all other times, we will continue to be a robot and an actress.

Amendment VI—1992—32 years old

This amendment was proposed and accepted when Jody started therapy following two years of severe asthma.

We amend our decision to never trust anyone, and conditionally allow ourselves to trust Dr. Jim, as he seems to listen and seems willing to help.

We will continue to "act" in all other situations.

We will continue to cut ourselves, make ourselves sick, and continue running away from the return of bad memories and bad feelings from childhood while in therapy.

Amendment VII—1998—40 years old

This amendment was proposed and accepted when Jody was working successfully and no longer frequently hospitalized, either medically for asthma or psychiatrically.

We amend our decision not to have feelings, as we have discovered joy in painting and going for walks.

We amend our decision never to tell each other our individual experiences, as it feels good to be friends with each other on the inside.

We amend our decision to "act" in *all* situations, as we have discovered it can actually feel good to be a nurse and to help others.

We amend our decision never to ask for help, as our doctors have helped us tremendously.

We agree to accept help, both in talking during therapy and in taking medication.

We agree to always and forever hate our mother for the horrible things she did to us.

Proposed Amendment VIII—2008—49 years old

The following amended rules of survival have been proposed. They will be experimented with and then voted upon following a trial period, after which Amendment VIII will be accepted or rejected.

We conditionally amend our decision never to have feelings based on our ability to tolerate feelings at any given time. We will allow ourselves to have feelings as long as they are not overwhelming. Should any feelings, whether good or bad, start to become overwhelming or intolerable, we will use the following strategies to regain a feeling of safety:

> Draw animals, apples, or still life.
> Paint a landscape.
> Listen to music.
> Go for a walk.

We conditionally amend our decision to never have friends. We will allow ourselves to only be as close to a friend as we feel comfortable, and should this begin to feel threatening—whether we get scared, or if our friend actually does something hurtful—we will allow ourselves the following strategies to regain a feeling of safety:

> Withdraw for a period of time, for as long as we need to.
> Hug a teddy bear at home.
> Confront the person about the hurtful incident.

We conditionally amend our decision never to talk honestly with people. We will use the following strategies to balance honesty with safety:

> Assess each individual person with whom we are talking, to determine if they are safe.
>
> Decide in advance what we think that person is capable of hearing or understanding.
>
> We will not prematurely divulge graphic details of past abuse to friends, as people probably are not capable of hearing this.
>
> Talk to our doctors when we need to discuss the past.
>
> Withdraw for a set period of time if we appear in any danger of getting hurt from being honest with someone.

We amend our decision to always punish ourselves for being social, with the stipulation that since socializing is new, and can be overwhelming, we can take pre-planned breaks and spend private time to regain a feeling of safety.

We amend our decision to cut ourselves as a first defense.

The following strategies will be used for safety:

> Call our doctors.
> Take PRN medication.
> Draw some animals/elephants.
> Hug a teddy bear.
> Take a shower or a bubble bath.
> Listen to music.
> Remind ourselves we are in the present, not the past.
> Re-state a "Safety Contract" with either of our doctors.

Further amendments can be proposed as the situation warrants.

Part Two

TRAUMA LEADS TO ASTHMA—ASTHMA LEADS TO THERAPY

Why, Mommy, Why?

Living through early childhood abuse led me to develop nine alter personalities: Little Jody, Ronnie, Jenny, Jennifer, Jeff, She, Janet, The Little One, and Jessie. Although I was completely unaware of the alters prior to beginning therapy in 1992, they were the only reason I survived.

As a child, I heard voices in my head. I had no idea—no one did—that they were the voices of my alter personalities. It was a childhood marked by everything from a series of self-destructive behaviors—cutting myself with scissors and razor blades—to frequently running away from home and living on the streets downtown. I was picked up by the police on numerous occasions and taken to juvenile detention. When I was 13 years old, I was admitted to a state psychiatric hospital where I was diagnosed as schizophrenic.

The culmination of my self-destructive behaviors was a near-fatal suicide attempt at 17. I'd gone away to college and was living on campus, but I had no skills whatsoever for surviving in that kind of environment. I'd barely been there a month when I overdosed on my mother's psychiatric medication that I had decided to take with me, just in case.

I ended up in a coma for a week and the doctors didn't expect me to survive. But they didn't know—at the time neither did I—about the crucial part my alters played in helping me pull through.

When I came out of the coma, the doctors determined that I was not stable enough to remain on campus, so I was sent back home to live with my parents.

That's when I resolved—consciously and subconsciously—to change my life. Since even suicide did not work, and life was intolerable, I decided from that point on to live life as a stone statue.

"I have no feelings," I told myself.

And I believed it completely, without question. I became an actress whose one and only role was to play the part of a normal person. I began to keenly observe and study normal people, how they behaved, how they talked and interacted.

I also told myself, *"Nothing bad has ever happened to me."*

I repeated it in my mind like a mantra, over and over again, until I believed it absolutely. I was determined that no one, including myself, would ever know the truth.

The past was *gone*. My self-induced amnesia was complete.

Studying normal people, I realized I needed a job and a family of my own. Since I was so good at learning—I had always been a straight-A student—I pulled it off. At the age of 18, I got a job in a hospital. When I applied to a local nursing school, not only was I accepted into the program, but I was awarded a full scholarship for scoring the highest on the entrance exam out of all the applicants.

I married at the age of 20, and gave birth to my son two years later. I had been observing how married people behaved, and no one was the wiser. I was a very competent registered nurse working in a busy medical center, and I was admired professionally. I was a respected member of society. In short, I had a normal life.

No one knew that, inwardly, I was made of stone. My theme song was Simon and Garfunkel's *I Am a Rock*. The only genuine feeling I allowed myself was to love my son unconditionally. Somehow I knew how deeply important that was.

But the inner turmoil from childhood could not be silenced forever. After 14 years, the stone statue began to crumble. I was 30 years old when I first developed asthma. It was my mind and body's only way of saying, "I need help." It was also the catalyst I needed to start the long road to recovery.

In the summer of 1990, my husband, son and I flew to the Canadian Rockies for vacation. While we were in Canada, I started to run a high fever and I developed a respiratory infection. A doctor there prescribed antibiotics, but by the time we returned home, my condition had severely worsened. I was diagnosed with pneumonia in both lungs.

That was the first time I was medically hospitalized. Little did I know I had just opened a revolving door of medical and psychiatric hospitalizations that would recur every one to two months for the next ten years. During this entire rollercoaster period, I was never home for a period of more than eight consecutive weeks before being readmitted to the hospital.

Pneumonia soon developed into asthma, which spiraled out of control. None of the usual medications were helping. I was sent to specialists; I was using four inhalers and taking multiple oral medications and steroids. I was on Prednisone for a full year. Whenever my doctor attempted to decrease the dose, my symptoms returned with a vengeance. And Prednisone is *not* without side effects. I gained weight, my blood pressure skyrocketed, my feet and ankles swelled up. I was put on blood pressure medication. I went in for X-rays, CT scans, allergy tests, allergy shots, you name it. I was in and out of the hospital constantly.

The frequent hospitalizations began to take a toll on my marriage. My husband became frustrated and irritable. At one point when he came to visit me at the hospital, he was angry that I had forgotten to stock the house with Kleenex before being admitted. Insignificant? Maybe. But that was the straw that broke the camel's back.

I couldn't hold it in any longer. I felt completely out of control. At home one afternoon, a sense of urgent desperation washed over me.

I paged my only doctor at the time, my pulmonologist, Dr. Rita.

When she called me back, I told her, "I don't know what to do. I'm reading the PDR to see which of my medications will interact right to kill me if I take an overdose."

She said, "Don't do anything until I call you back. I'll call you in a few minutes."

Within 10 minutes, the phone rang. She said she had spoken to a colleague, a psychiatrist, who advised her to hospitalize me right away. She did so under the pretence of an asthma flare-up so she could call a psychiatrist named Dr. Tony in for a consult.

I phoned my husband, Mark, at work. I didn't tell him I was suicidal, only that I was very depressed and Dr. Rita wanted to hospitalize me.

The psychiatrist saw me the next morning at the hospital. I know I cried, but I can't remember about what. He prescribed an antidepressant, Wellbutrin, and I was discharged in three days.

My outpatient appointments with Dr. Tony did not go well. We didn't talk much. He gave me a cognitive therapy workbook, and during our sessions, we simply discussed my assignments. The medication he put me on made me shaky and anxious.

I was suicidal again within two weeks.

I paged Dr. Tony, but that was futile. His office said I would have to wait until the following week to talk to him.

I couldn't wait. I was desperate.

I had no choice but to call my pulmonologist again.

I explained to her how it just wasn't going well with the psychiatrist. Fortunately, Dr. Rita had one other alternative: Maybe I could see a psychologist she knew.

"Sometimes, a psychologist is easier to talk to than a psychiatrist," she said.

And that's how I met Dr. Jim, who would be my therapist for the next 17 years.

When I called to make my first appointment with him in April of 1992, I was a little apprehensive. I didn't know what to expect. But, somehow, there was a small seed of hope. Could this man help me?

When we met for the first time, I had the distinct impression that he could.

He could be a friend, an "ally." He took the usual history—family, friends, etc. He asked me if I had ever been in therapy before or if I'd ever been on any medication. I answered "no" to all of his questions. I was sure it was the truth. My amnesia was complete. I was in complete denial that I had ever been in a state psychiatric hospital at 13 and attempted suicide at 17 only to be psychiatrically hospitalized again.

I told Dr. Jim that I came from a "normal" family. My only problem was unrelenting asthma and some marital problems. "My husband keeps getting angry at me and blaming me for things I didn't do. But nothing *unusual* has ever happened to me," I said.

At the end of the session, Dr. Jim simply smiled and said, "Well, I think I can help you. I have asthma myself, and I have experience with chronic illness—my wife has chronic rheumatoid arthritis. Let's plan to meet once a week."

After that first consultation, he recommended I start taking antidepressants. As I was no longer seeing Dr. Tony, and therefore did not have a psychiatrist at the time, Dr. Jim consulted via phone with Dr. Rita (my pulmonologist) and she gave me prescriptions for Elavil, an antidepressant, and Ativan, for anxiety.

I started seeing Dr. Jim once a week.

But the asthma episodes continued, as did the transgressions in my marriage.

・・・・・

AFTER I HAD BEEN SEEING Dr. Jim for several months, the first of many crises occurred. My husband became angry with me one evening for misplacing some important papers (I have no memory of doing this). The incident triggered childhood memories of guilt and blame… but I was *totally unaware of this subconscious connection.*

All I knew was that I should die for what I had done.

The next day at work, I called Dr. Jim in a suicidal crisis. I had the means to kill myself and a well thought out cover story to tell my husband.

I told him I was so depressed that I didn't even feel my body was my own. I had washed my hands at work in the sink and, looking at them, I had the strangest sensation they were *not my* hands. He told me later that this was "depersonalization" and it meant I was in a severe depression.

I was to get off work at 3:30 p.m. Dr. Jim said I should come into the office at 6 that evening. But ten minutes after hanging up, Dr. Jim called me back and said I should come to his office directly after work.

I arrived there at 4 p.m. We talked for a very short time. Then he got up, telling me he had to check on something.

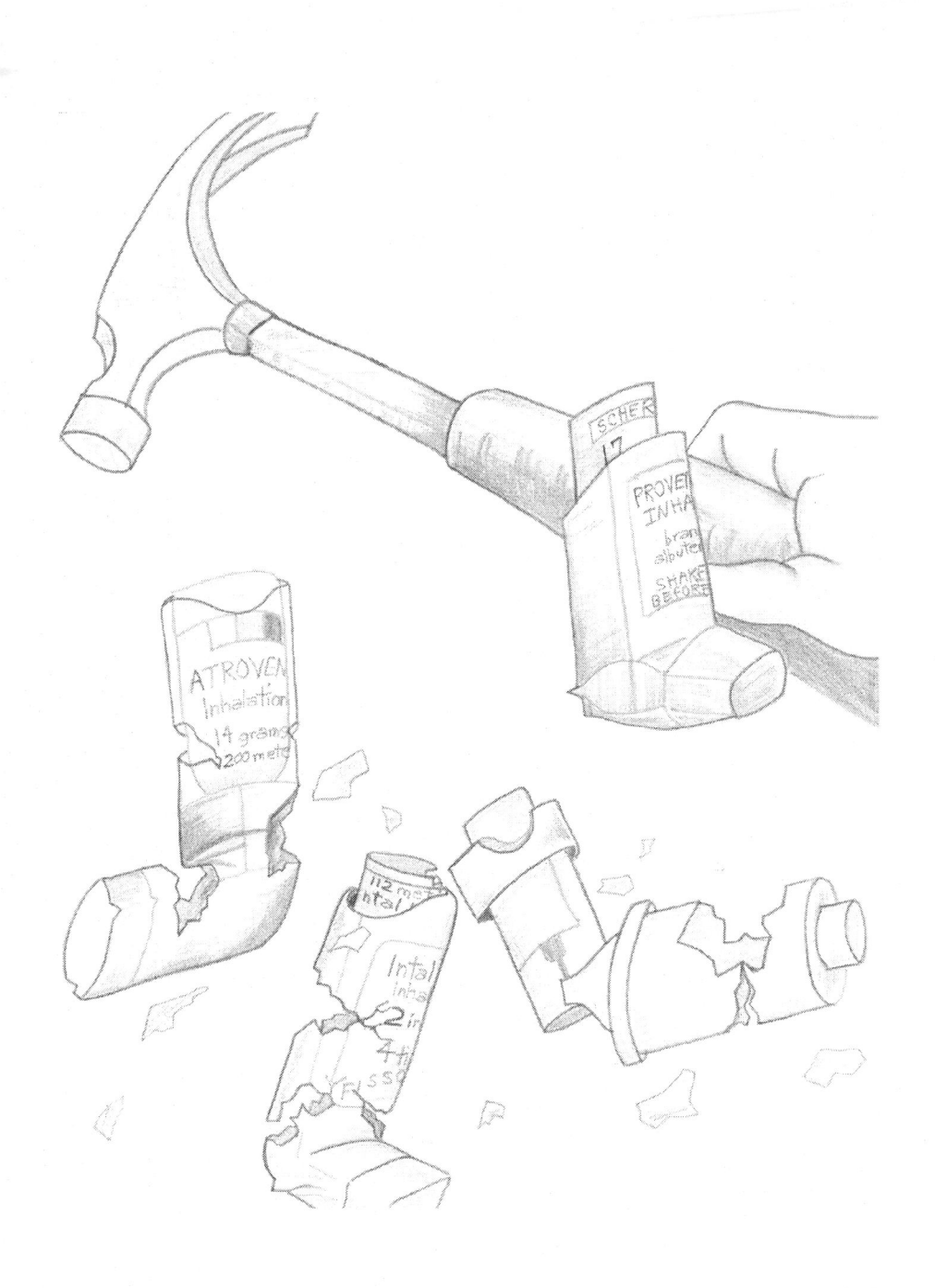

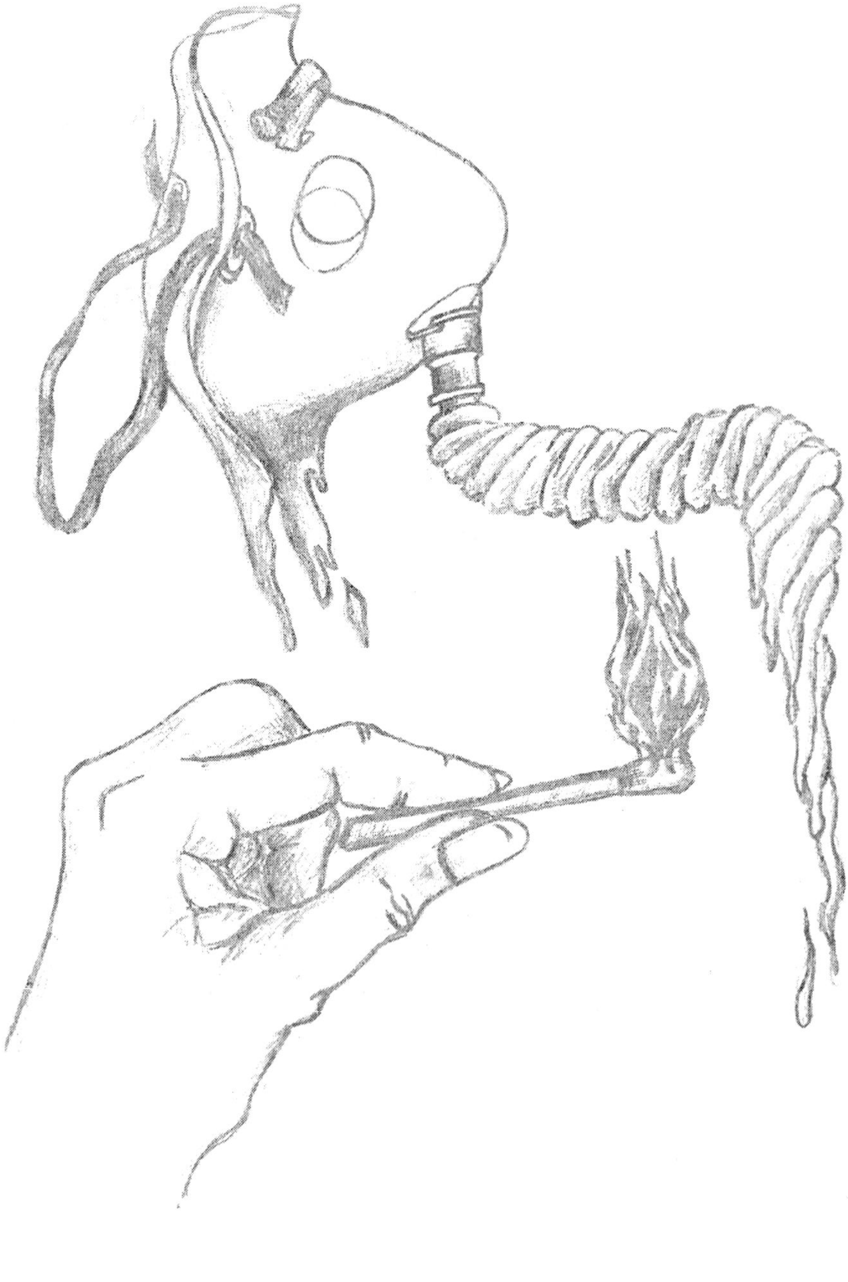

When he returned a few minutes later, he was accompanied by police and ambulance personnel.

Dr. Jim had called 911. He was sending me to the hospital!

I slowly got up and went with them. I was shocked by all of this.

Riding in the back of the ambulance, still wearing my nurse's uniform, I was completely silent. I could hear the siren of the ambulance. I could feel how fast we were going as they whisked me past traffic to the hospital.

But it was all a blur. All I felt was shock.

In the emergency room, I know I was asked to sign a voluntary admission form, which I did. I was doing everything by rote. No feeling, no emotion, no thought. Just do what you're told.

I was given a wrist ID band with the name of a doctor I had never heard of before: Dr. Nathan.

What would happen next? I didn't know. I didn't care.

There were locked double screens covering all the windows in my room. I was on the psychiatric unit of a private hospital.

I called my husband to tell him where I was, but I don't remember much of that conversation. What I do remember is that later that first evening, around 9 p.m., Dr. Jim appeared on the unit to see me. I was sitting on my bed in my room when I suddenly saw him standing in the doorway.

Everything came pouring out. I cried and cried. The tears just streamed down my face, years of pain pouring out. I had no conscious thought of what I was crying about, but the stone statue had been broken. The pain was about to begin.

I spent 19 days on that unit. That was to be the first of 25 psychiatric hospitalizations within the next eight years. From 1992 to 2000, I was in the hospital more than I was at home.

That first stay was an eye-opener. People were getting shock therapy, and being put in quiet rooms and held down in restraints.

Dr. Jim came to see me every day. And my new psychiatrist, Dr. Nathan, saw me three day a week.

I don't think I made a lot of progress during that first stay, but I did numerous therapeutic writing assignments for Dr. Jim.

One of the most important assignments came when Dr. Jim told me to write a letter to god about how having asthma felt.

But I didn't believe in god *and* I didn't have any feelings that I was aware of. That's when Dr. Jim introduced me to the concept of writing *as if* I had feelings. This would prove to be a crucial first step in recognizing that I actually did have feelings.

During this hospitalization I learned what a "contract for safety" was.

When I was finally discharged, it was on the following conditions, as stipulated by the contract:

Agree to keep myself safe.

See Dr. Jim once a week.

Attend group therapy once a week

See Dr. Nathan once a month for medication review.

I still had no memory of the past, no knowledge of the alters, or of any past abuse. I only knew I was depressed and suicidal.

But something about my talks with Dr. Jim made me feel that maybe he could help me. Help me with what, I didn't know.

Just help me.

So I met with him weekly and attended group therapy in his office every Monday night. At the group I was a zombie. It must have been six months before I said one word. But I was never pressured to talk. Throughout my entire therapy process, Dr. Jim has let me go at my own pace.

We spent the first few months of therapy discussing day-to-day events, mostly revolving around my asthma treatments and medical hospitalizations. What started innocently enough, though, was that I began drawing pencil sketches about my asthma. One drawing was of hands holding inhalers, another was hands holding pills and pill bottles ... to take an overdose. The recurring theme was "hands."

Because of the hands, I suppose, Dr. Jim ventured to ask, "Did your mother or father ever hit you?"

"No," I said.

My resolve to forget the past was still intact. Yet I continued drawing the hands. After several more months of these sketches, I had my first flashback.

I remembered being in the hospital when I was probably four years old, being on an exam table and crying, upset that I had urinated on the table. I sketched this picture and brought it in to Dr. Jim. I still couldn't remember how or why I would have been in the hospital at that age, but Dr. Jim didn't pressure me.

He said, "You'll have the answers in your own time."

Part Three

BEGINNING TO REMEMBER

"You'll have your answers."
—*Dr. Jim*

Why, Mommy, Why?

THE CONSTITUTION

Ratified in 1963 – five years old

We, Jody and the sum of all the alters, in order to form a union for survival, provide for a common defense, and promote safety for all, do establish this Constitution for daily living. We will live according to its laws, which is the only way to ensure our survival in a world of abuse and terror.

These laws shall include, but are not limited to:

Never go along with what Mother tells us to do.

Stay as far away from her as possible.

Stay with Dad as much as possible for safety.

Never show any feelings—especially never show that the beatings hurt us in any way.

Allow whichever alter is best suited to the situation to be in control.

The alters must never tell each other what they had to do while in control.

Each alter may decide the best course of action for survival in each situation.

Always rebel in the face of adversity.

Always use dissociation for safety.

* * * * * * *

IT WAS A SATURDAY MORNING.
I was washing my hair at home in the kitchen sink and, as I saw the water going

down the drain, I was transported back in time to when I was four years old, sitting naked in the bathtub at my parents' house. It was one of those old-fashioned white tubs with porcelain feet. The tub wasn't filled up, but the hot water was running.

My mother was kneeling on the bathroom floor beside me. In her hand was a shiny, silver metal cup.

Mother was repeatedly filling the cup with hot water and pouring it between my legs on my genitals. The water was *so* hot. It hurt, but I dared not scream. Somehow I knew better than to let my mother know she was hurting me. I watched as the water swirled down the drain of the tub.

REMEMBERING THIS, WITH MY HAIR dripping wet in the sink, I paged Dr. Jim in a panic.

I was getting flashes of images. First it was the bathhtub ritual with my mother. Then I saw myself lying in bed with my father's leg over me. There was a brown blanket. I was moving back and forth between these images, over and over again.

Dr. Jim returned the page immediately, and I told him first about the images of being in a bathtub.

"What was she trying to do?" he asked.

"I don't know," I said.

I could see the pictures in my head as clearly as if they were happing right now before me, but my resolve to forget the past prevented me from remembering the circumstances surrounding the events.

I told Dr. Jim about the image of my father's leg on top of me in bed.

"I think I may have slept with my father," I said.

And that was the crucial first step in breaking down my wall of forgetting. There would be countless times I would regret relinquishing my resolve—the resolve I had developed when I was 17 to live as though nothing bad had ever happened to me.

"I want you to come see me today," Dr. Jim said.

Even though it was Saturday, I knew he had a home office where he sometimes saw patients on the weekend. There were several people waiting to see him when I arrived, but he made time for me.

During that session, Dr. Jim gave me some colored pencils and paper and a simple assignment. He told me to draw what I would consider to be a safe place. This concept was new to me and somehow it seemed scary. But I set to my task.

I drew a mountain with a single, beautiful green tree on top. The mountain was surrounded by a deep gorge, which no one could possibly cross over to get to me.

That safe place became my sanctuary for a long time during our scary therapeutic journey together into the past.

My First Safe Place

Hold on tight to the prism.

Concentrate on Personal Power.

Know this will separate the present

    from the past.

Dr. Jim also asked me to draw an image of "personal power."

I drew a prism with the sun inside of it—keeping in the sunlight. I would keep this drawing in my wallet for strength.

For the next several months, I was plagued by unrelenting flashbacks of being sexually abused by my father, and, worse, of being psychotically, verbally, and physically abused by my mother.

Dr. Jim and I discovered together that the flashback I'd had of urinating on a hospital exam table was from Children's Hospital, where I'd been hospitalized when I was four.

I'd been hospitalized several times as a small child for seizures and, after a long work-up, the doctors found out that the seizures were secondary to severe, repeated urinary tract infections. The doctors started me on seizure medication, which I was to be on for the next ten years.

At the time, I'd undergone numerous diagnostic procedures, x-rays and exams to determine the cause of my urinary tract infections. The true cause, sexual abuse, would not be discovered until decades later in therapy with Dr. Jim.

Sexual abuse was not even considered in the early 1960's.

I obtained my hospital records from Children's Hospital while I was in therapy for proof of these hospitalizations.

The hospital had become a safe place for me as a child. I immediately became attached to the doctors and nurses there. I still have the drawings I made as a four-year-old of the doctors with wings. They truly were my guardian angels.

Little did I know these early hospitalizations helped me in ways I couldn't imagine. First, they helped me determine my career choice as an adult—I decided then that I would become a nurse—to help people as those nurses helped me. Also, my positive experiences in the hospital set the stage for my being able to feel safe enough in hospitals as an adult to do the tremendously hard work of therapy that was to come.

The realization that my dad could have been abusive was totally unacceptable. *I could not accept it.* I loved my dad. He represented "safety" for me. I didn't yet remember all the abuse from my mother, but I did know that if I was with Dad, I was safe. After all, he called me his "Little Dolly." I had such loving memories of him. But the fact I had slept with him (in his bed with the brown blanket) could no longer be denied.

I also knew that if it was true, I had to kill myself.

I struggled with the idea of suicide for a few weeks. Dr. Jim suggested I come in for a session one evening after work with my husband, Mark.

During that session, Dr. Jim suggested I be admitted to the hospital so that I "wouldn't have to keep struggling with myself."

At least there was no 911 call.

Dr. Jim's idea made sense to me. It would be a relief to finally stop struggling. So my husband drove me to the hospital.

That was my first stay at Meadows.

The memories of Dad were so fresh, so raw, that what happened next was not surprising. Meadows Hospital required all new patients to have a physical exam. And my psychiatrist, Dr. Nathan, had a colleague, Dr. Bruce, who was a medical consultant at the hospital.

So, the staff took me off the unit in the morning for a physical.

The memories of my dad touching me, the flashbacks... I couldn't control it. By the time they brought me back to the unit, I was crying inconsolably. The staff didn't know what was wrong, and I was in no state to tell them. Luckily, Dr. Jim had just arrived on the unit to see me, and he explained to the staff why I was so upset. I didn't blame Dr. Bruce. As a matter of fact, I learned to trust him, and he is one of my medical doctors to this day.

Because of the unrelenting flashbacks, Dr. Jim taught me to do "grounding" techniques. But it was hard to do any kind of productive therapy while I was trapped in the past. I couldn't think logically. The feelings were overwhelming; I felt like I was actually back in 1963. At times, I even thought I could *see* people from my past. These were not hallucinations, just flashes of images, and they occurred everywhere: in the hospital, at home and at work.

The grounding techniques that Dr. Jim and I used were a prelude to further therapeutic techniques to come. During future hospitalizations, I'd learn to use cognitive therapy, psychodrama and art therapy and pacing techniques. But I still had all of this in front of me.

For now, I just needed to be stabilized.

We used several methods to try to keep me grounded in the present. First, I tried telling myself what year it was, over and over again.

"It's 1992, not 1963. 1992. 1992."

Physical sensations helped, too. I would hold tightly on to the chair I was sitting in and remain focused on and aware of the floor beneath my feet. Then I would use visual cues—looking around my environment, whether in the hospital or at home—so I could see that I was *not* back at my parents' house.

I would repeat my age aloud: "I am 34 years old and I am an adult. I am not a child."

In addition to these techniques, I made myself small, credit card-shaped "reminder cards" that I could carry with me in my purse. These were a lifesaver, especially when I was at work. I carried cards with pictures of my safe place, my prism of personal power, and cards with written reminders of the present.

Burning Dad's Bed

Destroying Dad's Bedroom

I also visualized a large, red stop sign. When I felt like I was being drawn into a memory, especially when I started feeling that I was "bad," I would picture this stop sign as an "alert" signal that I needed to return to the present. I also drew it on a card to keep with me.

Although these techniques were not one hundred percent effective at stopping the flashbacks, they set the stage for my future work of separating the past from the present, and of finally being able to find, objectively, the meaning behind my memories. Over the next ten years of therapy, I made many of these cards to remind me of everything I was learning.

I was in the hospital for a month that time. My task was to take my dad "off the pedestal" I had put him on for so many years. I struggled with images of sex, penises, abuse and love. How could all of these be reconciled?

Dr. Jim suggested I write a story about all of this happening to another little girl—not me. What would I think of her?

And then the true trauma began to come out. It wasn't the sexual acts with my dad that were making me so suicidal—but the fact that I believed it was all my fault. And my mother was to blame for that.

Day after day, morning after morning, after I would get up from being in bed with my dad, (my parents never slept together; my mother always slept on the couch), my mother would yell and rage at me, "Good girls don't sleep with their fathers!" And then she'd beat me with the leather strap she kept in the closet.

Even worse than that, she told me over and over again that she had "Little People" that lived under the stove in the kitchen. They were watching me day and night. They wrote down everything I did and said, and reported it back to Mother.

After I remembered the "Little People," whenever I had a session with Dr. Jim—whether in the hospital or at his office—I would crawl around the floor checking the heating vents looking for the Little People who could report back to my mother what I was saying to Dr. Jim.

I was totally terrified that these Little People had followed me into adulthood and could still report back to my mother that I was *bad*.

Dr. Jim had to move his office at one point. On my first visit to the new building, I arrived 30 minutes early to "scout it out." I parked in the lot and carefully, slowly, walked all around the outside of the building several times to make sure there were no Little People lurking in the shadows. Dr. Jim's office was on the second floor, so I made sure to investigate the inside hallways, too. Only then did I feel safe at his new office.

* * * * * *

My mother envied the relationship I had with my father—something she didn't have. She hated me for it, and tortured me mercilessly.

My parents had stopped talking to one another. If they had anything to say, they did it through me.

"Jody, tell your father this," and "Jody, tell your mother that."

Otherwise we lived in total silence.

During those years, my mother tortured me on a daily basis. It wasn't just the beatings. She had, in her top drawer, some dental instruments. She would make me sit, with my legs spread apart, and poke at my vagina with a dental pick, while holding a mirror and making me watch.

She continued the bathtub ritual to "cleanse me of my sins" with my father.

During those years, I knew I lost time. Switching to one alter after another was the only way to survive. Ronnie, Jenny, She, and the others each underwent their own individual torture. None of us was aware what the others were going through.

There were only two constants: Dad, and knowing Mother was someone to avoid.

I avoided her as much as I could—even though that meant getting in worse trouble. One of my chores was to dry the dishes when my mother washed them after dinner. But even when I was very young—I was probably five or six now—I was so certain my mother was evil that I thought I would be poisoned if I touched a dish she had put down in the sink.

I tried to run—into the living room, the bathroom, anywhere to avoid touching those dishes. When I couldn't run anymore, and couldn't stand the beatings for refusing to dry the dishes, I coped the only way I knew how: After she put the dish down, I would count to ten in my head to let the poison wear off. And then I would gingerly pick it up and pray to Jesus that I wouldn't be poisoned and die from touching it.

As my mother continued her emotional and physical torments, I began to draw pictures. I did drawings of me killing her, shooting her with a gun as she slept. I knew no other way to escape. Then I drew pictures of Jesus, praying for him to rescue me. I put all of these drawings in a special wooden box under my bed. I called it my "Jesus Box."

One day my mother found that little wooden box of crayon drawings and tore them all up in a fit of rage. I would not draw again for 30 years.

Since I couldn't draw, and Mother continued the abuse, I turned to Colleen, a little girl who lived next door. I had to tell someone.

One summer day, sitting on the front stairs of my house, it all came pouring out. It did not have the effect I had hoped for.

Colleen told her mom. Her mom confronted my mother. What happened to me?

Out came the leather strap. Then I was locked in the garage until the next day—with no food or water—and, of course, I had to urinate on the cement floor.

I learned then that it was a mistake to be honest with people, *and*, it was a mistake to try to have friends.

AT FIRST I WAS RELIEVED when I was old enough to start going to school. I thought at least I'd be safe there. There would be no beatings, no leather strap, no sexual abuse. But school was never as easy as I hoped.

The voices in my head plagued me throughout the school day, and I repeatedly got reprimanded by the nuns for "spacing out" or "daydreaming." There were papers I turned in to the teachers with different names on them.

I excelled in my classes and I aced every test, but that didn't count for much. In the second grade, I turned in a science report with the name "Ronnie" on it. I had no explanation.

The parent-teacher conferences never went well. I had hoped to be praised by my parents for doing well in grammar school—for getting A's in every subject. Instead, my mother focused on my bad behavior, daydreaming and writing "stupid names" on my homework assignments.

I was beaten and locked in the garage after my parent-teacher conferences.

I was completely devastated. Even trying my best was not good enough.

Nothing I did was right. I was bad no matter what—even with straight A's.

· · · · · ·

AFTER BEING REPEATEDLY HOSPITALIZED FOR my chronic urinary tract infections, I was followed by a urologist.

My mother would take me downtown on the bus to his office. Sometimes, his exam made me feel like I had to urinate, and the feeling would last for hours. The problem was, my mother always wanted to go shopping at the department stores after my appointment.

It was absolute agony. I felt so badly that I had to go to the bathroom. The whole time we were in the store, I'd keep saying, "I have to go to the bathroom!"

My mother was annoyed, and she took her anger out on me. First she yelled at me, sometimes hit me, and said, "No! You're not going to the bathroom! What's wrong with you?"

At long last, we would take the bus home and finally I was allowed to use the bathroom.

Between having to go following the doctor visits and not being allowed into the house until I urinated in the backyard, I learned early in life that there was

*The hole that I feel is real. It is deep. But the hole is not "me."
It is the impression left by a heavy stamper my mother used.
The stamper left behind a hole and also caused cracks, splits,
because it was so heavy. But because she pushed so hard,
it created some things I might never have had.*

something inherently bad about urinating. My fear about "having to go" would follow me into adulthood. Whenever Mark and I would go anywhere, I had to know at all times where the bathrooms were, or where the next rest stop was along the highway, just in case.

As a small child, all I knew was wanting to go to the bathroom made Mother angry, and that meant I was bad. I learned to fear ever telling anyone when I had to use the bathroom, and I learned to fear the physical sensations in my body whenever I needed to go.

All of this became so ingrained that it led to more problems at school. During bathroom breaks, I'd walk in the line with little girls going to the bathroom, but I would not go in. I was too frightened that I might do it wrong. Because I didn't go with the other kids, a short time later, I had to go. But my mother had taught me it was wrong to ask. I tried desperately to hold it, as I had downtown, but eventually I couldn't hold it any longer. There were many times I wet my pants.

Once, all the kids were lined up at the teacher's desk to get their papers back, and I couldn't hold it. The urine dripped onto the floor, making a puddle in front of the teacher's desk. I didn't say anything, and we all returned to our seats.

The teacher finally saw the puddle, and she was furious. She demanded to know who had done it. I was scared and embarrassed to say the least. I did not confess. But I was found out when she checked each student's chair to see which one was wet.

The other kids teased me, but that was nothing compared to my mother's reaction. The school had called her, and she was waiting for me at home with the leather strap.

"What's wrong with you? You *never* act right!" she yelled. I hung my head, endured the beating and again knew there was definitely something wrong with me. I was bad on the inside. There was no other possible explanation.

When my mother developed some medical problems, she constantly reminded me it was my fault that she was sick.

"If only you knew how to behave, I wouldn't have to go to the doctor!" she railed at me.

Her heart problems were my fault. She needed shots for her eyes—which was my fault.

In time, my father began to tell me the same thing, "Your mother wouldn't be sick if only you knew how to behave."

I was never able figure out what I had done wrong to cause her to get sick. So, the seeds were sown—*I was just bad, inherently bad.*

THE TIDE OF ALL THESE memories continued to swell, day after day.

"I'd rather die of pneumonia than remember all of this about my childhood," I told Dr. Jim on the phone one day.

I awoke the next morning with a severe asthma attack, and had to go to the emergency room. I was hospitalized with asthma for two weeks. Dr. Jim called me every day I was in the hospital to see how I was doing. He was my lifeline.

I couldn't stop the past from returning. Memories continued to wash over me as flashbacks, nightmares, and panic attacks. I could barely function. Trying to sleep at night was impossible. I clung ferociously to the memory of being safe in my dad's bed. On the nights I did not sleep with my dad, my mother would tuck me in, and she would tell me bedtime horror stories of witches, candles, and caldrons.

I took Ativan five or six times each day. Dr. Jim had a pager at the time and, on some days, I would beep him a half-dozen times each day.

At work, I was plagued with flashbacks. I would "keep it together" until my breaks or lunch, when I would page Dr. Jim. He always called me right back.

We did "safety measures" over the phone to help me cope. He helped me relax with breathing exercises or counting backward from one hundred.

He also had me visualize a "thought vacuum." It was a huge vacuum connected to my head that would suck out all the images of the past, and lock them in a safe that couldn't be opened until our next session.

The vacuum also connected to my eyes to drain away the tears so I could go back to work. These techniques worked for awhile. Sometimes I called him at 10 p.m. to do these exercises to help me go to sleep.

Once I paged him at 3 a.m., *terrorized* by nightmares of my mother's face and those angry eyes. Just the sound of his voice calmed me down. That was the only time I had to page him in the middle of the night.

Dr. Jim always said to me, "Remember, I'm here for you."

I have always held on to those words.

* * * * * *

I FELT COMPLETELY VULNERABLE. THERE were triggers everywhere I turned.

I was sure I wore a sign on my forehead that said, "I am an incest survivor" and that my co-workers could see everything I was going through. Of course, no one knew or even suspected a thing. I was very good in my role as an actress, and I was a very competent nurse.

But memories, flashbacks and feelings of blame continued to plague me at work. I remember going to work one morning and finding that a patient I had been caring for over the past several days had died during the night.

My Heart on Ice

I panicked and paged Dr. Jim.

I confessed that I was to blame for this man's death.

"What did you do to him?" Dr. Jim asked.

I was taken aback by his question. "No," I said. "He died because I've been doing bad things by telling you all of these secrets. I'm not supposed to be telling you all this stuff."

It took a very long time for Dr. Jim to convince me there was no magic that could make me cause someone's death by revealing "secrets."

There were even triggers involving Dr. Jim himself. Early in therapy, Dr. Jim had taken some time off and was hospitalized for a minor surgical procedure for a hernia. I went into a suicidal crisis because I was certain I was to blame for his medical problems—just as I was the cause of my mother's illness.

I talked with his partner, Dr. Susan, on the phone. She asked me if my crisis was related to Dr. Jim being in the hospital, but I was too frightened to admit it to her.

I dismissed it, "No, I know a hernia repair is a minor surgery and that he'll be okay."

I never admitted to anyone my secret fear that he was going to die because I had told him secrets about myself, my mother, and my father.

* * * * *

Amendment I—1969—11 years old

This amendment was proposed and accepted when Dad abandoned Jody at age 11.

> We have the right to run away from home as often as the need arises, as there is no longer any safety at home.
>
> We have the right to try to enlist outside help—by attempting to talk to the police, priests, nuns, doctors, social workers, anyone.

My dad abandoned me when I was 11 years old and started my period.

"We can't play anymore," he said.

I suppose it was smart on his part, not wanting to get me pregnant. But I was *devastated*. I felt emotionally abandoned. I was left more vulnerable and unprotected from Mother than ever before.

When I remembered that day at Dr. Jim's office, I bolted out the door, ran down the stairs, and into the parking lot.

Dr. Jim ran after me.

I told him I wanted to run into the street and get hit by a car. We talked for a while in the parking lot until he managed to calm me down.

That's when I started hearing the buzzing in my ears. And it just wouldn't stop, for days. Then I remembered the details about the day my father abandoned me.

We lived in an apartment and, that summer, the whole building was infested with flies. That finally explained where the buzzing was coming from.

My mother said, "Your father won't play with you anymore because you're garbage! That's why there's all these flies. Because you're garbage!"

I bolted from the house and climbed up a tree at the park.

Decades later, I asked a relative about the flies. He confirmed that there was an infestation of flies. The people in the apartment next door were living in filth.

But I had believed my mother without question. I was the garbage the flies had come for.

After my dad abandoned me, I began running away from home and cutting myself. Between the ages of 11 and 13, I ran away countless times.

There was nowhere at home that I was safe from Mother. Dad's bed would no longer protect me.

I was scared and I had to relieve the pressure of the voices in my head. One afternoon, I took my mother's sewing scissors into my bedroom and cut X's into my ankles—four X's, two on each leg. The relief I felt was undeniable. From then on, I was "a cutter." I would use cutting for decades, whenever I felt trapped or overwhelmed.

After that first incident, I put my socks back on, to hide what I had done.

My mother found out, got angry at me and beat me with the strap yet again.

But, what she was angry about was *not* the cutting. She was enraged at how hard it would be to get the blood out of my socks!

This first episode solidified for me the relief one feels though self-harm, and I learned to bandage my wounds to keep the blood off my clothes.

Years later, in therapy, when more bad feelings returned, I found new and creative ways to harm myself. I continued the cutting—with razor blades at home and, when I was in the hospital, I'd use paper clips, staples or the corners of tissue boxes.

I also made myself deathly ill once by taking a cold shower and then sitting wet and naked in front of a fan for 20 minutes in the middle of winter. Other ways included sticking pins and feces in my vagina—"mirror" images of what my mother had done to me with the dental pick.

As far as running away goes, mostly I would get on the subway and end up downtown. I lived on the streets for days at a time, with money I'd stolen from my parents' dresser drawer. In the end, the police would always pick me up and bring me back home. At that time, I had not yet come to believe that life was completely hopeless—and I tried, on numerous occasions, to tell the police what was going on at home and to ask for their help. They never believed me, and they always brought me back home.

One time, I decided not to tell them my name when they picked me up, so they took me to juvenile detention. It was scary, but still better than going back to my parents.

I met a very friendly social worker at juvenile detention, and, since I hadn't yet made it a personal law never to talk to anyone, I told him everything. I thought he would help me. Instead, he called my parents, and I ended up back home, greeted by another beating with the leather strap.

When I was 12 years old, I knew I had to get far away. One Saturday, I stole some money from the drawer and headed downtown on the subway. I wandered around until I came to a Greyhound station.

I knew I couldn't spend all my money on a ticket, so I settled on a cheap one—a ticket to St. Louis, Missouri. It was about a six hour trip, and I think I slept most of the way. I was exhausted.

When I arrived in St. Louis, I wandered around downtown and got something to eat. But I was scared and I was still hearing voices in my head. More than that, I didn't know where I was, what I was going to do, or what would become of me. I had no skills to survive in a strange city, and I didn't know a soul.

So I returned to the Greyhound station where I spent the night on a bench.

In the morning, I felt defeated. Home was horrible, but it was the only place I knew. So I bought a ticket back, and was welcomed home by a beating from my mother.

All my father said was, "Why didn't you just tell me you wanted to go to St. Louis? I would have given you the money."

What a strange thing to say to a 12-year-old.

How could he not see my desperation?

I kept running—but there was really no place to go. My mind desperately searched for somewhere—anywhere—to turn.

Since school seemed a safer place than home, I turned to the nuns. I went to a Catholic grammar school, and one of my teachers, Sister Marie, seemed to be especially kind. Could she help me, I wondered?

I began spending extra time with her. I would stay after school. I spent my lunch periods with her. I needed her desperately.

One day she invited me to the convent for dinner. I was so excited!

I thought I was saved.

At the convent, I felt safe and began pouring my heart out to Sister Marie.

Suddenly, I found myself back at home being beaten my mother's strap yet again. I didn't know what had happened. I had lost time. How did my mother find out? How did I get home? Had my parents picked me up? No matter—I endured the beating.

My mother was in a rage, yelling something about me *never* joining a convent and how terribly *bad* I was for going there in the first place.

I spent the entire next day locked in the muddy crawlspace beneath our house, and was made to urinate on the ground like an animal. My mother was determined that I learn my lesson about how *bad* I was.

But I *still* hadn't learned not to try to reach out for help. I was a survivor.

After the incident with Sister Marie, my mind turned to the priests at our church. I wondered—since they listened to confession, and could absolve you of all your sins, maybe a priest could give me penance for being such a bad child, and then Jesus would forgive me. I remembered how, years before, I had longed for Jesus to save me.

I was scared, anxious and apprehensive—but, on Saturday, I walked the four blocks to the rectory of our parish where the priests lived, and I rang the doorbell.

The secretary buzzed me in.

"Can I talk to a priest?" I asked.

Father John and I sat together and I told him my sins: How I was a bad girl for having sex with my father .... How I must have been really bad because I gave my mother heart problems and eye problems .... How my mother told me it was my fault that our neighbor's house burnt down because I didn't behave right .... How I lit evil candles with my mother to make bad things happen.

Ronnie, Jenny, Jennifer—all the alters—and I took turns describing each of the atrocities we had committed. I'm sure Father John was unaware he was talking to a whole group of kids. We went on and on about how bad we were. I finally said I wanted to know if Jesus could ever love me again. He then told me to wait there for a moment.

When he returned, he said my mother was on her way to pick me up.

Even the priest would not help me. Even God had abandoned me.

. . . . . .

I FELT COMPLETELY ALONE. I didn't have anyone to talk to. I did not have my dad. I did not have God. And I had learned from my mother never to have friends.

I also was sheltered completely from anything that happened outside of the family. For example, in eighth grade, in the 1970's, our teacher told us we could all bring in some music. One of the girls brought in *Joy to the World*.

"Why did you bring in a Christmas song?" I asked her.

Everyone laughed at me. I had no idea that there was a new song out called

Joy to the World that had nothing to do with the holidays. I really knew nothing of current events, nothing outside of my house and school.

There were other traumatic episodes as well during those tumultuous years after I lost my dad. Since I had no experience with people outside my family, and I was never taught the basic rules of trust or safety, it's not surprising that I fell victim to other types of abuse.

One episode occurred during my first year of high school. I had to walk six or seven blocks from the house to the bus stop to get to school. One day, on my walk, a car pulled over and a man offered me a ride. As I thought men were always safer than women, I immediately accepted, and he drove me to the bus stop without incident. The next morning, I rode with him again. On the third day, he pulled over a few blocks before my bus stop, turned off the car and started kissing me, touching me, trying to take off my clothes. My experience with my father taught me what would come next. I don't know how, but I was able to bolt from the car.

I froze, then I ran. He did not follow me.

I never told anyone about the incident, and started taking a different route to school. Fortunately, I never saw the man in the car again.

No one had ever taught me not to trust strangers, and I believed the incident was my fault. Again, I learned that there is no safety.

I had a very similar experience shortly after that. I spent some Saturday afternoons at the movie theater. It didn't matter what was playing. It was just a way to get out of the house. Since I had no friends, I'd go alone.

I was sitting in the theater half-watching the movie, half just "spacing out," when I felt a hand on my leg. It was the man sitting next to me. I froze.

I didn't know what to do. I got up and bought some candy. Not knowing any better, I returned to the same seat. It happened again. So I went to buy more candy. It happened several more times—until I ran out of money—and then I left the theater.

I knew nothing about safety. Again, I never told anyone about the incident, as it was just another example of how I caused something bad to happen.

* * * * * *

Amendment II—1971—13 years old

This amendment was proposed and accepted when two years of trying to get help failed, and we ended up in a state psychiatric hospital.

> From this point on, it will no longer be acceptable to reach out to other people, as this only results in further punishment and further reduction of safety.
>
> We must never talk honestly with other people again. We must never have true friendships.

Should a friendship inadvertently arise, we must sabotage it to maintain safety.

Only Jeff will interact with Dad.

We will continue to never show feelings. We will allow Jennifer to have control, since she has no feelings.

We will, from this point forward, live life as a stone statue.

Should any feelings inadvertently arise, we will cut ourselves with scissors or razor blades to eliminate them.

RUNNING AWAY AND LOOKING FOR help only served to land me at the state psychiatric hospital when I was 13.

On one of the occasions when the police picked me up downtown and I tried to tell them all what I was running away from—what was going on at home—and how there were voices in my head telling me things, they took me to the hospital.

There, I was diagnosed as schizophrenic, and placed on powerful antipsychotic medications, Thorazine and Haldol.

In addition to making me a zombie, there were terrible side effects: my neck and other muscles would stiffen and shake. I couldn't control my movements. It was a horror story.

Adolescents went to unit D. Some of the children there were catatonic, others were screaming. There were restraints and shots. There were shock treatments. Intermittently, over the next several years, this would be my home.

Decades later, whenever Dr. Jim was going to hospitalize me, I would have terrible flashbacks of this place and beg him: *please*—don't send me to D!

I was hospitalized many times during adolescence. Between hospital stays, I continued running away from home. Sometimes, I'd even run away from the hospital.

My first and only experience with drugs occurred once when I ran away.

I was downtown one afternoon, walking the grounds near a museum when I saw a girl about my age. She was smoking, and she called me over. We introduced ourselves and at first we just made small talk.

Jackie was in high school. So was I.

She told me she'd like someone to do pot with. I knew what it was, but had never tried it. I was a little apprehensive, but thought, *why not?*

As we smoked pot together, I began to feel really strange, dizzy at first. But then it seemed to relax me. After smoking several joints, I began to get giddy and felt sort of confused. The next thing I knew, we were at a coffee shop sitting at the counter and talking. I started talking about incest, in general at first, and then I started telling her about me and my dad.

I was laughing about it. Everything was funny to me.

We certainly got stares from the other customers, since I was laughing and talking so loudly. Jackie said she had to go, and I was left alone thinking about what had just happened. An alarm bell went off in my head. I remembered that I'd promised myself never to talk honestly about anything that happened at home. But even though I was pretty shocked about what I'd told Jackie, I still thought it was funny.

The rest of the day was a blur. I was still laughing when evening came, wandering the streets downtown.

I was stopped by a police car, and they asked me some questions. All I remember is that I told them I lived at the state hospital. They took me to the police station where I wouldn't tell them my name. I just kept telling them to take me to the hospital.

By now, the drug had worn off and I was terrified of returning home, knowing what I'd revealed to Jackie. I knew from experience the consequences that awaited me for telling secrets. So, even though the hospital was a frightening place, at least I wouldn't suffer at the hands of my mother. And so, I was admitted again to D.

Because of what pot made me do, made me talk about, I vowed never again to do any drugs.

I don't know how, but finally one of the doctors at the state hospital recognized how terrorized I was at the thought of going home, and he said I needed a different place to live.

I'm not sure what they knew about the psychology of self-destructive behavior back in the early 70s, but my history of constantly running away from home and cutting myself at least allowed the doctors to recognize that there was a legitimate problem.

The doctors told my parents I could be discharged only if different living arrangements were made. My parents had no choice but to comply.

There was no Department of Children and Family Services back then, so it was arranged that I would live with my aunt. Aunt Maureen, who had always been a very kind person, agreed to let me stay with her for the next six months. My parents agreed to give her money for my room and board.

Living with Aunt Maureen was a really strange experience. As their children were now adults and had moved away from home, it was just Aunt Maureen, Uncle Matt and me living in the house.

I was not at all used to this new kind of living environment. The first truly odd thing I noticed was that Aunt Maureen and Uncle Matt *talked* to each other, unlike my parents, who never spoke.

There was also no one who yelled at me, and no one who beat me. I wasn't constantly being told I was bad or not behaving right. There were no candles being lit, no bathtub rituals, and no bedtime stories of witches and caldrons.

The three of us ate breakfast together and had dinner together at night.

Evenings were quiet times—filled with soft conversation, TV, and sometimes, dessert. Despite this calm, I remained on guard.

I never once spoke of my parents or anything that went on at home.

After living there for several months, I began to associate Aunt Maureen with safety. Years later in therapy, my doctors would sometimes have me visualize Aunt Maureen and her safe home.

This was to become a great asset in therapy as a self-soothing measure. As I never once needed to run away or cut myself while living with Aunt Maureen, visualizing her house sometimes helped me avert a self-destructive crisis.

The time with my aunt was a reprieve from abuse, but my lessons had been learned. Never talk to people. Never again try to get help. Never show feelings. Never have friends. Remain a stone statue.

And, throughout high school, I succeeded. No one suspected I was a statue, no one knew about the alters. There were a few girls in my classes who tried to be friends with me, but I had learned the lessons from my mother all too well. So, I did the only thing I could: Sabotage!

I was creative. For example, one of the girls who seemed to like me was Polish. I spread rumors about her to the other girls that she was "a big, dumb Polak!" That effectively ended the "friendship." Although I never meant to hurt anyone's feelings, I felt I had no choice. I had to be safe.

And so I was alone.

During my final year of high school, after I returned home from living with my aunt, I ran away again. But I did not end up in the state hospital this time. Our family doctor recommended to my parents that I be placed in a psychiatric unit at a large university hospital in the city. We received a referral for a private psychiatrist.

They did some medical tests and an EEG. The doctors thought maybe the seizures I'd suffered when I was four and five years old had caused some brain damage. All the tests came back normal.

During a conversation with my mother and me, my latest psychiatrist pointedly asked Mother if I had ever slept with my father. Where he got this idea, I don't know. I had learned not to talk to people anymore and had never told him a thing about my parents. My mother gave him a surprised look and emphatically said, "NO! Of course not." The subject was never brought up again.

I didn't utter a single word about my past to any of the doctors or staff. I just bid my time until I was released. This place was a far cry from the state hospital, and the staff were friendly enough, but years of no one listening, no one believing me had taught me well. My resolve to remain silent was unbreakable. Knowing I didn't want to return home, I tried various ways to hurt myself. This was the first time I actually felt suicidal.

At first, I resorted to what I knew—cutting. I looked everywhere on the unit for weapons to use. I found small sharps, but these only made superficial scratches. I tried starving myself, refusing to eat or drink for several days. The staff, however, noticed what I was doing and told me I would be transferred to the medical unit for IV fluids if I didn't start eating and drinking.

Nothing worked. I had no choice but to cooperate with the staff and feign recovery. Eventually I was discharged and I returned home feeling depressed and defeated.

AMENDMENT III—1976—17 YEARS OLD

This amendment was proposed and accepted following a failed suicide attempt at age seventeen.

- As life is intolerable and even suicide does not work, we will, from this point on, live life as an "actress."
- We will completely forget the past and live life as though nothing bad has ever happened to us.
- We will survive by keenly observing other people and "acting" as a "normal" person based on those observations.
- We never will be honest with other people and will avoid friends at all costs.

I DIDN'T HAVE MY DAD. And I didn't have my aunt. I was in a black hole. I had nowhere to turn.

At 17, I had finished high school, but was still living at home.

Since I had always excelled at school, I decided to go to college, and was accepted at an out-of-town university.

After moving into the dorm, I was completely lost. I was completely alone except for the voices in my head. I had no skills for making friends, and Ronnie and the other alters had no skills for surviving among college students. I was on a mental rollercoaster of panic and intolerable loneliness.. When I wasn't in class, I spent all my time alone in my dorm room or walking by myself on campus. I couldn't even bring myself to eat with the other students in the cafeteria. I ordered pizzas delivered to my dorm room and finished everything so no one would know I was there by myself.

How I wished I could have called my dad, but I knew that was futile. I couldn't go back home, and I couldn't survive on campus. I had learned years ago that asking for help was useless—though I toyed with the idea of the campus health center.

Finally, one night, I decided my only option was suicide.

I had brought a bottle of my mother's psychiatric medication with me, and, with resolve, I took the entire bottle while walking on campus.

The next thing I knew, I was in a hospital in intensive care.

Years later, after meeting the alters, I learned that when I swallowed the pills, Ronnie took control and got me to the campus health center where she told them what I had done. Ronnie had made one last, desperate attempt to reach out for help. And saved my life.

I was in a coma for a week, and was not expected to survive. But, somehow, I pulled through, and came out of the coma.

This is when the alter Janet came into being. She was 17, and would remain 17 and suicidal for the next 30 years.

Janet never turned 18 because I'd missed my eighteenth birthday while I was in a coma in intensive care. It would take years of intensive therapy to convince Janet it was now safe to relinquish her hold on suicide and okay to move on with life and have her eighteenth birthday.

After being discharged from the intensive care unit, I was transferred to the psychiatric unit for a week. Although I was still depressed, I was not actively suicidal in the staff's opinion, so I was released.

From there, I went back to my parents' home yet again.

It was November of 1976.

The next six months were a blur. I was literally in a void. Occasionally, I would listen to my mother's record albums, but that did nothing to help me. Depressed to say the least, I sat on the couch most of the day, literally doing nothing. I was home alone with my mother during the day, and by this time we rarely spoke, or interacted at all.

I had no options. Even suicide did not work.

It was after six months of living in this void that I made my resolution to completely forget the past and become an actress.

My resolve was uncompromising.

I vanquished the past. I vanquished the voices.

I banished all feelings.

I "acted" as a normal person for the next 13 years—until the acting took its toll and I developed severe asthma in 1990.

Amendment IV—1979—20 years old

This amendment was proposed and accepted when Jody got married and received a nursing degree.

We will observe how married people behave and "act" accordingly.

We will function as *one person* in the workplace in order to hide our true identities and to survive.

SINCE MY PARENTS DIDN'T TALK to each other and I had no friends, I had no experience with normal behavior. So, I resolved to get a job, "observe" people and imitate everything—the way they talked, acted, behaved, and interacted—everything down to their facial expressions. I knew I could do it!

I put an employment application in at a local hospital. I only had a high school diploma, but I was willing to do whatever work was available. Within in two days, the director of the respiratory department called me. He asked if I was interested in working for him as a respiratory therapy aide. This mostly would involve transporting patients by wheelchair to and from the department.

I took the job, and it was the perfect learning lab for me. There were seven or eight other young people working in the department, and I was a keen observer. No one knew I was an actress. I quickly picked up on when to talk, what to say, when to smile. I had all the cues I needed.

Concurrently, I applied to a two-year nursing program. I received the highest grade on the entrance exam and was awarded a full scholarship.

Now I would be a *normal person!*

The other issue was that, even though I was working and going to school, I was still living with my parents. So, I thought, what else do normal people do? They get married. They start a family. And that's when I met my future husband. I had been working at the hospital for a few months when two new guys were hired. Both were single. I knew something was meant to be.

Mark and I started talking, and it turned out that, like me, he was in school, and his school wasn't far from my parents' house.

I had no previous experience with dating, so I was at a loss as to how to begin. I began taking an interest in his school… and said I was out walking one evening to the drug store next to campus. I suggested maybe the next time I was at the drug store, I could see him after class?

It worked! Mark invited me out for dinner one evening after class at a restaurant across the street.

I was anxious, but I keenly observed him, keeping in mind all the lessons about interacting with people that I had learned at work.

I played my part well. After just a few months of dating, Mark proposed.

I couldn't believe it! Finally I would get out of my parents' house!

Although I had never dated before, I wanted to have sex with him... I wanted to "go all the way."

Mark refused. He didn't believe in premarital sex. I didn't know why that was so important to him, but it was.

I was not consciously aware of any memories of my dad. All I knew was that if a man cared about you, he had sex with you. Was I doing something bad? Was there some reason he wouldn't have sex with me? I wasn't consciously aware of why I was thinking this way.

I tried to convince Mark, but it never happened.

My other desire was to get married as soon as possible. I finally had my way out within my grasp, but Mark wanted to wait to get married until I graduated from nursing school. That would be another 18 months. I felt that I couldn't wait. I had to get out of the house. Again, I didn't know why. I had no memories of anything bad, I just *knew*: I had to get out!

I asked Mark several times to move up the wedding, but he refused. Waiting was very difficult, but at least I was out of the house for work, school, and for our dates.

We dated for two years, and were finally married a month after I graduated nursing school with an RN degree.

Nursing school had not been easy for me. It was a two-year, year-round program with very few breaks. Although this was good for keeping me away from home the majority of the time, it was exhausting—the classes, the labs, the homework, the papers.

Although I excelled in nursing school, getting mostly A's in all my classes, the hardest class for me was pediatrics. We did our clinical rotation on a pediatric unit at a local hospital. It was really difficult for me to deal with those sick kids. I think it was the crying, the pain they were in, and the sadness. On the outside, on the surface, I had no clue why this bothered me. But, somewhere, on a deep emotional level that I could not admit, these kids were evoking my own memories of childhood pain and tears. And this transferred into my work in the classroom. It became increasingly difficult to concentrate, to focus on learning pediatric conditions and illnesses. I finally made it through the course with resolve.

Pediatrics was my lowest score on the RN board exams. I vowed never to work in pediatric nursing, without even knowing why.

Being an actress both at work and at school was hard enough. And, as I said, the classes were grueling. There were several times I thought about quitting. On those occasions, my fiancé, Mark, was always there for me. He encouraged me to keep going. He was a constant support. Without him, I never would have earned my degree in 1979.

Mark knew there was something wrong at my house. He could see immediately that my parents never spoke to one another. He saw that my mother treated my father like dirt. He saw that my father would "go to China to avoid a conflict." But Mark couldn't even begin to suspect the scope of the problems. And, at that point, neither did I. All I could do was to tell Mark over and over, "Don't say anything." I knew enough to understand how important it was that the fragile veneer be maintained.

After we were married, I got my first nursing job on a medical and surgical unit at the same hospital where I'd been working while in school.

Life appeared fairly normal for several years.

I excelled at my new profession. I was becoming very proficient at being an actress at work, and I even made some *pseudo*-friendships. I call them *pseudo*-friendships because there were no feelings involved. I became very good at small talk by observation and repetition, but I shared nothing of myself. I remained a stone statue on the inside, while appearing calm, relaxed, friendly and competent on the outside.

Being young, and being "friendly" with the other nurses, I soon became part of their group of friends and started going out with them after work. We went to bars and drank—I suppose that was what young people did. But drinking was not good for me. Sometimes it made me laugh—and I knew somewhere deep inside that laughter was dangerous.

Subconsciously, I was still following the laws in the Constitution that told me to avoid feelings and friendships. So I stopped seeing these girls, and to this day I avoid alcohol like the plague.

I did continue working, though, from 1979 until I went on disability in 1994.

* * * * * *

Amendment V—1981—22 years old

This amendment was proposed and accepted when our son was born.

> We amend our decision to never have feelings. We allow *one* feeling: Love Rich unconditionally.
>
> At all other times, we will continue to be a robot and an actress.

My son was born two years after we were married. I knew nothing about raising a child—but somehow I knew this child must be loved.

I allowed myself one single, solitary feeling: to love my son. To this day I don't understand how or why I was able to do this. Somewhere, deep in my soul, I knew a child needed to be loved, deserved to be loved, and he *would* be loved.

I had no memory of how abusive my mother had been to me, but I knew I would be a good parent. I read books; I trusted my instincts. And, I believe I was a good mom. I treated my son with respect; I treated him as a person. And I knew he felt loved.

Since I had no previous experience with either raising a happy child or being a happy child, I relied on other people to guide me, to let me know if I was doing things "right."

And, for sure, he was loved by everyone who met him. Relatives, other mothers at the playground, everyone invariably told me, "You have such a happy boy!"

And, most importantly, he seemed to have no difficulties talking to people—adults or other kids—and no problem making friends. I'd know I was doing something right when I'd watch him playing happily with the other children at the playground.

As he grew, he excelled in school as well. I remember many parent-teacher conferences where I was told, "He's a joy to have in class."

I began therapy when he was only 11 years old, and began my recurring hospitalizations when he was 12. Although I was completely absorbed in the therapy, I was still aware of how this could affect him. In the beginning, in 1992, I tried to cover up what was really going on by telling him I was hospitalized for asthma. But I soon realized this was wrong and that truth was the best policy.

I have tried to be as honest with him as possible, and I've always hoped my absences did not traumatize him too much as he was growing up. And I always have, reminded him, and still do, that he is loved. Today I think we have a really good relationship. Given what he had to endure with my illness, he has grown into a wonderful young man.

I don't know how I was able to make this amendment to the Constitution regarding actually allowing a feeling—love—but whatever the cost to me, it was definitely worth it.

Part Four

DISSOCIATION—DISABILITY—HOSPITALIZATIONS

Why, Mommy, Why?

Amendment VI—1992—32 years old

This amendment was proposed and accepted when Jody started therapy following two years of severe asthma.

> We amend our decision to never trust anyone, and conditionally allow ourselves to trust Dr. Jim, as he seems to listen and seems willing to help.
>
> We will continue to "act" in all other situations.
>
> We will continue to cut ourselves, make ourselves sick, and continue running away from the return of bad memories and bad feelings from childhood while in therapy.

Although I succeeded in my acting roll until I developed asthma in 1990, I started not coping well in 1987 when my dad passed away. That fateful day will forever be etched in my memory. My dad had called me one evening saying he wasn't feeling well—probably "coming down with a cold or flu." He told me he had taken some cold medicine, but just didn't feel well. I had a gut feeling something was wrong, so I called his doctor to schedule an appointment. As it happened, his doctor was out of town—and I was put through to the doctor on call at the hospital. He told me to bring Dad into the hospital tomorrow and he would meet us in the E.R.

The next morning, I had the day off work, so I took my son on the bus to my parents' house. My mother would watch him while I took Dad's car and drove him to the appointment.

As Dad was putting on his shoes in the bedroom, he said to me, "I'm dying." It was eerie, and I was taken aback. But I said, dismissively, "No, you're not."

I was tense, but still a stone statue. The drive to the hospital seemed endless.

We parked in the hospital lot, and Dad and I walked across the street. But, before we got to the door, he collapsed, grasping a tree for support.

What should I do?

Sure, I was a nurse, but this was Dad. I panicked! I saw someone coming out of the hospital, and yelled for help, "Get me a wheelchair!"

Suddenly, I found myself in the E.R. filling out paperwork.

The orderlies put Dad onto an E.R. cart and took him to be examined while the staff directed me to the waiting room.

It was a very short time later when I heard overhead, "Code Blue—E.R."

People scurried into the E.R.

It was Dad!

Within a few minutes, a nurse came out and told me Dad suffered a major heart attack, but they had revived him.

"Can I see him?"

"No, we need to get him to the ICU."

In fact, I'd never see him alive again. I was never able to say goodbye.

"Code Blue—E.R."

Again! I knew it was Dad.

Apparently, now they had him on life support and were transferring him to the ICU. Again I was stuck in the waiting room.

No one knew what was happening except me. My mother was at home with my son, and my husband was at work. Another nurse came out to tell me they needed to do an emergency procedure, to insert a pacemaker.

"Code Blue—ICU."

I sat in the waiting room for what seemed like hours. Then the secretary appeared with paperwork in her hands, and very calmly asked me, "What funeral home will you be using?"

"Funeral home?"

"Oh, you didn't know ... sorry," she said, and disappeared behind the door. A nurse then appeared and told me they were unable to insert the pacemaker and hadn't been able to revive him.

With his last words, he'd asked for me.

My heart was stone. I had no feelings.

I made phone calls by rote ... to my mother, my husband, my brother. One by one they arrived. My husband went to pick up my mother, and when she arrived, she signed the papers for the funeral home.

I had lost my dad again. I could not accept it, *would not accept it*. I couldn't cope with it. *No way.*

The rest of that day, and the following several days, I went with the family to the funeral home and we made all the necessary arrangements.

But I did not grieve the loss of my father. I was not sad. I was stone.

Over those next few days, I hardly spoke. I stared at my brother and my sister-in-law. I had no words and I did not cry at the funeral. Being an actress was of no help to me now.

After the funeral, I thought I could bury the second loss of my dad as conveniently as I buried the first.

But it took more energy to contain these feelings than I had anticipated. I became irritable, going to work was harder, and life in general was more difficult.

I lost Aunt Maureen the very next year, in 1988. I'd already lost her once in high school when I could no longer live with her. And now I would lose her to a heart attack.

It was one loss after another, and it was becoming increasingly difficult to cope. I had not recovered from the shock of Dad's death when I received a phone call at work telling me Aunt Maureen was in intensive care.

I was on and off the phone the better part of the day and was reprimanded by the nursing supervisor. Didn't she understand this was an emergency?

After work, I went directly to see Aunt Maureen at the hospital.

I learned she had undergone emergency bypass surgery, and had coded during the operation. Although she had advance directives of a DNR (Do Not Resuscitate), those orders weren't applicable during surgery. They had revived her.

By the time I saw her in intensive care, she looked really bad. She was weak, pale, and she could hardly speak. My mother was there, as well as my two cousins (Aunt Maureen's children).

Aunt Maureen asked to speak to me alone. Everyone else stepped into the hallway and Aunt Maureen pulled me close to her and said, simply, "It's time."

And, just like with my dad, my first reaction was to deny to myself that I knew what she meant.

I responded, "Oh, you want to know what time it is?"

But even more powerful than my urge to deny what I was feeling was the feeling that, deep down, I just couldn't bear a repeat of my dad's death—not being able to say goodbye.

So, I swallowed my pain, held Aunt Maureen's hand, and said, "It's okay to go. I know what you mean."

She smiled.

The others came back into the room, and I left. I didn't tell anyone what had happened.

And as soon as I arrived home, the phone rang. I learned Aunt Maureen died ten minutes after I left.

I attended her funeral—again with no words, no tears. I could not grieve the loss. Why did people feel they could tell me when they were dying?

Then, there was yet another loss.

The one person who had been helping me "keep it together" was Mark's mom, my mother-in-law. She was kind, not like the mother I was used to. She was, for a short time in my life, the mom I never had.

She passed away the following year, in 1989.

It was only six months later that, following this series of three major losses, I physically broke down, developing pneumonia and severe asthma.

* * * * * *

WHILE WORKING ON EARLY MEMORIES with Dr. Jim, I frequently doubted myself.

Did all of this really happen? How could my "normal" family have been so bad?

Dr. Jim had cut through the veneer I had erected after my failed suicide attempt. By 1993, I'd been in therapy for a year, but I still had no knowledge of the alters.

I doubted myself about being sexually abused by my dad, doubted whether I'd ever been beaten by my mother, couldn't believe my memories of the bathtub rituals, the dental instruments, urinating outside ... none of it. I needed proof.

I tried talking to my brother, but his only response was, "Well, it wasn't a normal family, and I don't want to talk about it."

I struggled with the idea of confronting my mother. I was afraid to, but I needed to know.

Dr. Jim and I discussed it, and I decided it was something I had to do.

We met at a restaurant. The conversation started out innocently enough—but soon all my anguish poured out. I screamed at her, as faces in the restaurant turned toward us, "How could you blame me for sleeping with Dad? How could you say all those things to a five-year-old little girl?"

I screamed; I cried.

Mother denied everything.

But something in me wouldn't give up that quickly. I asked if we could go back to the house. When we arrived at my childhood home, I went to the closet and got out the leather strap she had beaten me with so often.

"Here's the evidence!" I said.

Then she relented. She admitted everything.

She said, "You were *my* child and I was *your mother*. I had every right to tell you what to do. You were always a bad child, and it *was* wrong to sleep with your father!"

So, it *was* true. I had my validation.

That didn't make therapy any easier. Quite the contrary. The hardest part was about to begin. But at least I no longer doubted myself.

ABOUT A YEAR INTO THERAPY, I experienced my first episode of dissociation.

I was talking to Dr. Jim about being on the streets downtown when suddenly, I felt my mind slipping away. I couldn't stop it. I heard Dr. Jim call my name, *loudly*: "Jody! Jody! Come back!"

He startled me back into the room. That's when he explained to me for the first time what dissociation was.

I finally had an explanation for all those periods of lost time.

He explained that something traumatic must have happened to me, and said we should meet again the following day.

He scheduled me as the last patient of the evening to give us as much time as we might need. In fact our session would last until 10:30 that night.

The memory that surfaced was of being raped downtown, near a theater when I was 13. In Dr. Jim's office, I relived the entire experience. It was so traumatic that I was visibly shaking from head to toe.

The circumstances surrounding the events remained a mystery. Why was I downtown? How did I get there? I wouldn't remember those details until years later.

This episode of dissociation unblocked many more years and many more episodes of dissociative states.

And that's how I met the alters.

I WAS EXTREMELY UPSET ONE day during my session with Dr. Jim. It was a Friday, and we were talking about my mother and her obsession with candles.

One minute we were talking and the next thing I knew ... the session was over and I was crying. I didn't know what had happened. He told me we had to have an emergency session the next morning—Saturday—at his home-office.

For the moment, I was to stay with his secretary until I calmed down and was able to drive home.

The session on Saturday was a complete mystery to me.

I remember going to his house. I remember him saying, "I want you to relax."

And then he said, "I'll see you on Monday and we'll talk about it."

What was going on? I was scared.

The session on Monday was just as scary.

I sat down, ready to begin.

Then I looked at the clock and 20 minutes had passed.

"I tape recorded this for you," Dr. Jim said.

I listened to the tape recording of the past twenty minutes, which sounded eerily unfamiliar.

The Safe Room—We each had our own key.

There was a child's voice on the tape. She said her name was Ronnie and that she lived "inside." The voice was that of a frightened little girl. She said she knew me, and knew what happened between me and my dad, but that it never happened to her. She said that sometimes she watched what happened. She wanted someone to talk to, but she was scared.

"I can help you," Dr. Jim's voice said on the recording.

Then Dr. Jim stopped the tape. There was silence in the office. This was all too much to handle.

But just then he said something I'll never forget. "There's nothing wrong with you—its just that bad things happened *to* you." Those words got me through the worst of times over the next 15 years.

MEETING RONNIE, WE FINALLY HAD an explanation for how the sexual abuse began. Through Ronnie, I learned that it had started innocently enough when I was very young. I used to have repeated ear infections that hurt terribly. I couldn't sleep at night. I screamed because the pain was so bad.

Dad was caring, he was sympathetic. He began holding me so I could fall asleep. Then, this turned into a regular routine—instead of going to my own bed, I would crawl into his bed with the brown blanket, and he would hold me until I fell asleep. Soon, the hugging turned into kissing, and then into a routine of sexual behaviors.

Ronnie also said that she was as terrified of my mother as I was, but she insisted that my mother was *not her mother*.

Ronnie tried to protect me. Whenever my mother wanted me to go out of the house with her alone, Ronnie would scream and grab tightly onto a door frame.

"No, I'm not going!"

Mother literally had to pry her hands loose.

Although I still had no conscious awareness of her, she started printing messages to me and drawing pictures.

Her first drawing was of Dr. Jim—someone who could help her.

Ronnie was six years old and terrified of birthdays and candles. She said she would *never* turn seven. We didn't know why.

One of Ronnie's first memories was of going to my childhood friend Paul's funeral. Ronnie recounted to Dr. Jim that our friend Paul had died when we were five years old, and that she went to the funeral. Ronnie remembered my mother telling her about the ghosts at the funeral, and how she'd better learn to behave, or else.

Ronnie couldn't remember anything else at the time. When Dr. Jim asked her what had happened to Paul, she cried, frightened, and said, "I don't know!"

Neither Dr. Jim nor I knew or even suspected that later we'd meet another al-

Dr. Jim's Wind-Up Toy

DR. JIM

RONNIE

Mr. Bear

ter, "She," who was created to keep the memory of Paul death because it was too painful for either Ronnie or me to deal with.

During that session, when I first heard Ronnie's voice on the tape recorder, Dr. Jim gently told me my new diagnosis: Multiple Personality Disorder (as it was called in the 90s.)

It was not easy to accept. How could there be other people living *inside my head*? And, if there were, why didn't I know about them? At first, I vehemently denied it.

The dissociation he had told me about earlier made sense—I knew about "spacing out." But I did not, at this point, even remember that as a child I had heard voices in my head.

Dr. Jim phoned my husband a few days later and tried to explain the diagnosis to him. I don't think he understood it well at first—or maybe, like me, he simply couldn't accept it.

Dr. Jim continued having sessions with Ronnie, and he would then "fill me in" on what transpired.

After awhile, I could no longer deny the existence of her drawings, her printed notes to me. She was scared and asking for my help. I finally relented, and everything came unglued.

....

The journey toward accepting M.P.D. sent my life into a tailspin for the next two years. I met an array of nine alters, and was hospitalized, almost like clockwork, every other month for suicidal thoughts and behaviors.

To help alleviate some of the fear, and subsequent suicidal thoughts, Dr. Jim had me create a "safe room" in my mind where Ronnie and the other alters could go when they felt scared. I could go there as well. This room was a green prairie with beautiful flowers, a wooden rocking chair, and, of course, a teddy bear. But this prairie was inside a room surrounded by a big, strong, sturdy brick wall. And it had a door with a special keyhole. We each had our own key.

Dr. Jim also gave us a "safe toy" from his office. Once, when I was feeling very suicidal at his office, I pleaded, "Please—don't let me kill myself!"

He said, "Look around and pick out something safe you can take with you."

On the shelf of his bookcase was a small wind-up toy. I wound it up, and this little creature began walking around on the shelf. I was afraid it would fall off. But it stopped walking just before it got to the edge.

Dr. Jim said, "See, he knows just how far to go and when to stop."

He said I could keep the toy as long as I needed it. I have that small wind-up

The alters before therapy

toy on a shelf in my bedroom to this day.

There was also a teddy bear named Spike who lived in Dr. Jim's office.

I came to depend on Spike, holding him tight during every session.

That was how I first started to use teddy bears to help give me a sense of security and safety.

Sometime later, I found another Spike at a gift shop, so then I had my own Spike at home. Many times when my husband and I went out, I would bring Spike with me in the car.

One year for Christmas, my husband got me a bear, who Ronnie named Mr. Bear. Mr. Bear went everywhere with me—to therapy, out to eat, and was even admitted to the hospital with me.

I'm sure it must have looked strange for a 33-year-old woman to be carrying around a teddy bear, but he became my security ... and that outweighed anything else.

During the following years, my husband bought me a collection of teddy bears, which remains, to this day, one of my biggest comforts in times of stress or crisis.

JOURNALING WAS ANOTHER TECHNIQUE I used to help alleviate stress. Writing about issues allowed me to make some of my biggest breakthroughs throughout the therapeutic process.

Journaling became a lifesaver when I started meeting the alters. Everyone used the journals—writing notes and coloring with crayons. It was through journaling that we sometimes met each other for the first time, shared our experiences, and got to know one another.

I'd never had a journal or diary of any sort before starting therapy. The first time staff at Meadows Hospital handed me a blank journal when I was admitted, I was at a loss as to what to do with it. But there were writing assignments from the therapy groups and assignments from Dr. Jim, and soon the pages were filling up.

Over the years, I've written many letters in my journals as well—letters to my dad, my mother, my aunt—letters never meant to be sent. These letters allowed me to finally get in touch with feelings I'd kept buried for 30 years.

Now I was journaling every day, whether I was in the hospital or not.

I started doing "surveys" in my journal. For example, if Dr. Jim and I were discussing a topic I just couldn't understand, I would write about how other people might explain it to me—such as different staff members I trusted at the hospital, and Dr. Jim's partner, Dr. Susan.

Occasionally, I took a phone survey, calling several of these people to discuss the topic. I'd record their responses in my journal. I continued taking surveys for several years. Through other people, I was learning life skills I'd never been

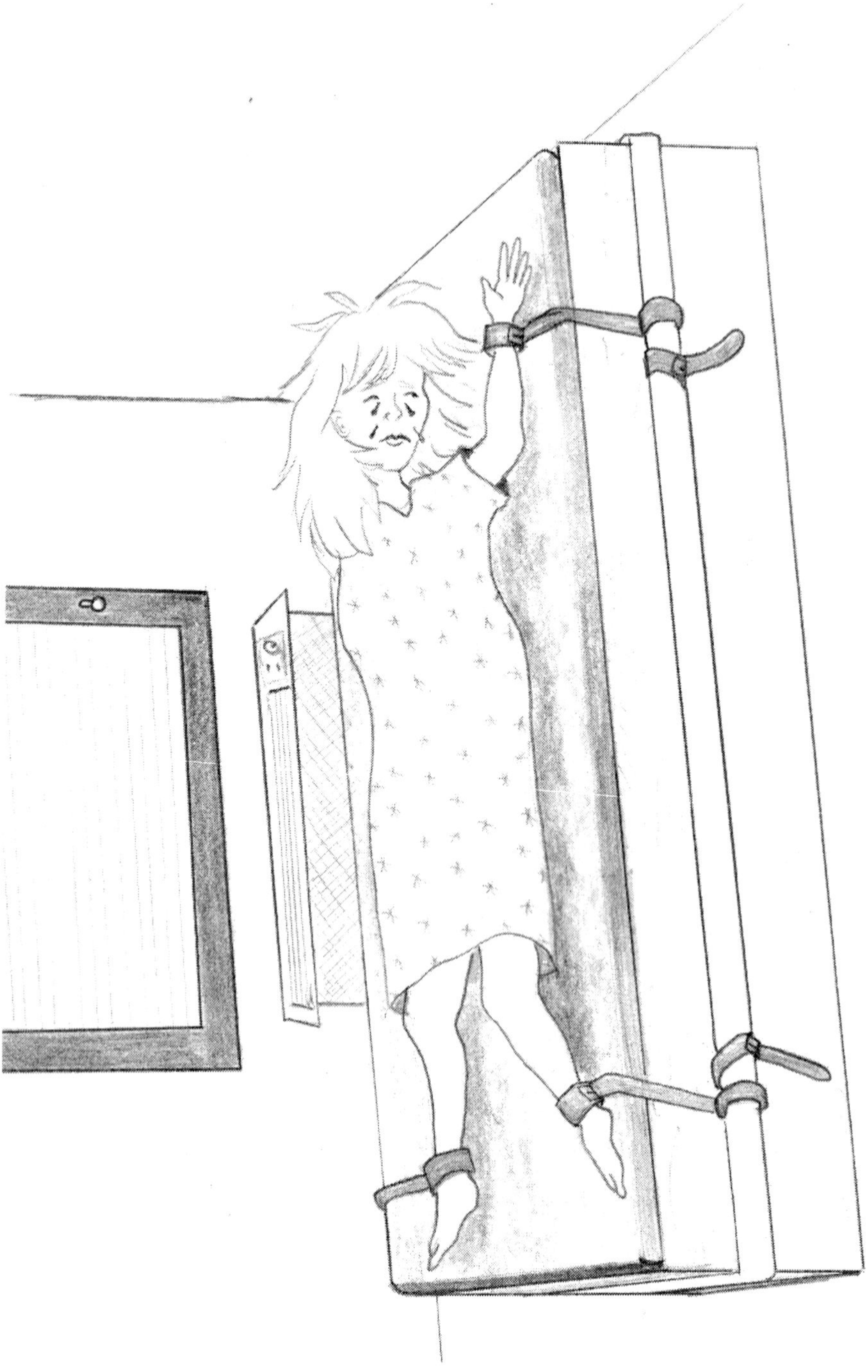

taught as a child.

Despite the emotional rollercoaster of meeting the alters, a really strange thing started to happen around this time: my asthma greatly improved. I was off steroids for months at a time.

It was an odd sort of tradeoff. I was no longer being hospitalized for asthma, but now I was being psychiatrically hospitalized for trauma.

In the summer of 1995, I was hospitalized during a prolonged flashback of my mother wrapping the leather strap around my neck to choke me.

My dad had rescued me, physically, but the emotional trauma remained.

The intensity of the memory was such that I felt an overwhelming desire to act it out. I continually tried to choke myself because I believed that's what I deserved. I tried to strangle myself with bedsheets, restraints, anything I could get my hands on.

My psychiatrist at time, Dr. Nathan, took this behavior as evidence that the antidepressants I was on weren't working. So, he had me stop taking my medication cold turkey.

I was back in the hospital in a suicidal crisis within a week.

My husband threatened to sue Dr. Nathan for malpractice.

Dr. Nathan had no experience with dissociative disorders. Antidepressants were the only medications he had tried. He had tried me on Elavil, Zoloft, Prozac, and Paxil, but nothing for dissociation.

Dr. Nathan had told me I couldn't take beta blockers due to my asthma.

Luckily, while in the hospital, I started talking to another patient who also had problems with dissociation. She told me about her doctor, Dr. Norm, who specialized in dissociative disorders. She told me there were plenty of medications for treating dissociative disorders that were not beta blockers.

Maybe, I thought, there was hope with Dr. Norm.

But would he take me on as his patient?

That evening, I asked the staff how to go about requesting a change of doctors. They had me put the request in writing, and, in a few days, Dr. Norm came to see me on a consult.

I remember that it was a long, grueling interview.

One of the things he asked me was, "Do you hear voices?"

Incredulously, I responded, "Do you want to know their names?"

I told him as much as I knew at that point about Ronnie and the others. It was exhausting—telling him everything I could remember about my history. In the end, he said he would be happy to be a consultant, but he didn't want to take a case away from another psychiatrist.

I pleaded with him to be my doctor—and I asked him to *please* call Dr. Nathan and at least discuss it with him.

I don't know what transpired during that phone conversation, but the next thing I knew, Dr. Norm was my new psychiatrist.

He immediately put me back on Paxil, and added Tenex and Risperdal. He gave me his office and answering service numbers, and drew up a safety contract, which both he and I signed.

The contract stipulated that if I called him in a crisis, he would get back to me within *one hour* if at all possible.

Given my past, and following my experiences with Dr. Tony and Dr. Nathan, it's not surprising I had a hard time with trust during those first few months with Dr. Norm. Although I felt safe enough to call Dr. Jim, I could not bring myself to call Dr. Norm when I was having a hard time.

During one of my outpatient appointments, I explained the problem to Dr. Norm.

He understood, and encouraged me to practice paging him. He told me that after I got home from my appointment, I should call his answering service anytime before 9 p.m.

I arrived home around 6, and struggled with calling him. Finally, at 8:45, I picked up the phone. Within ten minutes, he called me back. We talked a little more about how he had signed my contract, and told me again that I could depend on him. Slowly, I began to feel safe with him.

As time went on, I began to idolize him. He became, in my mind, like the doctors I had had at Children's Hospital who had rescued me from my parents—if only temporarily. He also became, in my mind, my father—who I turned to for safety from my mother. Dr. Norm became "a savior." I put him on a pedestal, just as my dad had been when I was a child. I was so dependent on Dr. Norm that I came to believe his words were law—even to the point of not acknowledging my own hard work.

I remember when Dr. Norm decided to try me on a new medication, Zyprexa, while I was at Meadows Hospital. At the time, Dr. Jim and I were working very hard on issues surrounding my mother always telling me I caused bad things in the world to happen.

One morning, I woke up thinking, "My mother tricked me!"

But later that day, when Dr. Norm came to see me on the unit and I shared my revelation with him, he said, "That's the Zyprexa working!"

I felt I had let myself down, that I hadn't accomplished anything. I believed only in what he said—not in my own hard work. It wasn't until years later, when I was able to take him off the pedestal, that I gave myself credit for all of my hard work.

Only years later did I come to realize how I had idolized Dr. Norm because, at the time, being so scared, feeling so bad, I desperately needed someone to rescue me. It wasn't until I had gained some confidence in myself, in making my own choices, in living the life I wanted, that I was able to see him as a doctor, not a savior.

* * * * * *

ALTHOUGH MANY OF MY HOSPITALIZATIONS were helpful, some were just as traumatic as my childhood. Because of frequently changing insurance benefits, I was shuffled back and forth between Alexandria Hospital and Meadows. Alexandria Hospital only had a general adult psychiatric unit, and the staff there did *not* believe in dissociation, much less in D.I.D./M.P.D.

At this time, I was not yet co-conscious with the alters. I was only aware of losing time and ending up in the "quiet room" on the unit, sometimes in restraints. The staff was always angry at me, yelling, "You're staying in there until you're done with your theatrics!"

I would overhear them talking amongst themselves about the show I liked to put on, pretending to be a little girl. Silently, I cried. My only reprieve, my only treatment there, were my sessions with Dr. Jim.

At one point I was put on High Risk Suicide Precaution. Somehow I had creatively unscrewed the metal coil insert from a roll of toilet paper and tried to kill myself with it. I was trying to escape from the abusive staff!

Eventually, my husband's insurance changed, and I no longer had to be admitted to Alexandria Hospital.

All of my subsequent hospitalizations were at Meadows.

Meadows Hospital, in the 1990's, had the advantage of offering trauma-specific groups. I was in Grief and Loss Group, Survivors Group, Psychodrama, as well as some others.

Of all the times I was hospitalized, my stays in Intensive Care at Meadows Hospital were the most productive. The staff members on that unit were unbelievably helpful. I will always be thankful for the head nurse, Kathy, and a psychology technician, Don. They kept me safe as much as possible, but most importantly, treated me with respect. I always got the feeling from them that I would survive these hard times. They gave me confidence; they gave me a feeling of self-worth. And since many of my symptoms stemmed from my mother's message that I was *bad*, their believing in me truly was the best therapy. They gave me what my parents never had.

Kathy was always willing to talk—on the unit, and even when I was in restraints. Kathy was kind, helpful and supportive—no matter which alter she was dealing with. It was a far cry from the abusive staff at Alexandria Hospital. All the alters

The Fountain

learned self-respect from Kathy.

And, as Kathy knew I was a nurse, too, sometimes we would talk about my work and "compare notes" about nursing. She helped me keep in touch with the real world and not get totally lost in childhood memories.

Don, the psychology technician, was always around to help me with my therapy assignments from Dr. Jim. I would write in my journal several times a day, and Don would read over what I had written and we would talk about it. Don would help me take breaks, too. All the staff at the hospital knew what a hard worker I was—to the point of working on so many issues that I would overwhelm myself. Don taught me that it was okay to relax, to take a break. He would play games with me—cards or board games. And this was when I learned the important lesson of pacing myself.

Because I've always dived into my work, both as a child and as an adult, I would sometimes get overwhelmed by journaling and other therapies. Dr. Jim and I soon came to understand that at times I was overwhelming myself with my ambition.

In considering pacing, a group that also helped me deal with this was Goals Group. This group met at 9 a.m. on Mondays, which helped me and the other patients schedule our therapy work for the day and the coming week. We learned to set "SMART" goals for ourselves. SMART goals were: S—Specific, M—Measurable, A—Attainable, R—Realistic and T—Timely.

Doing this helped me break down my therapy into small, more manageable pieces. For example, it was too broad to say, "I'm going to work on not feeling suicidal."

Even though that was exactly what I was working on through the group, I learned how to break this goal into parts that could be dealt with using specific, realistic techniques. The idea was to explore *one* aspect of each issue at a time.

My first task was to figure out the reasons I felt suicidal. Using the techniques I'd learned, I realized there were three reasons. 1) To punish myself for doing something wrong; 2) To run away from feelings; and 3) It was my last resort for staying safe from my mother.

The next step was to examine the pros and cons, as well as alternatives, to each of these thought processes.

I learned to work slowly and on one thing at a time.

I used the concept of SMART goals throughout my therapy, both in and out of the hospital. Especially while working with an alter who was feeling *bad* when some new memory arose, I broke the work down into manageable pieces.

I firmly believe that pacing is a very important aspect of trauma therapy.

All of the groups at Meadows helped me tremendously. But one that deserves special mention was the art therapy group led by an excellent art therapist, Marie. We did drawings, collages, and other artwork. It came easily to me since, even as a child, I had drawn what was important to me—the doctors as angels at Children's Hospital, the drawings of Jesus when I wanted him to save me. I remember one drawing in particular that I did in the group. It was a drawing of a beautiful fountain, with waterfalls streaming out from several different levels. This symbolized all of the alters working in unison.

Marie also taught us to do collages. I'd never tried this before, but I dived in head first. I always found pictures and phrases from magazines that seemed to fit the issues I was working on. Even when I was so depressed or scared that I couldn't find the words to speak, I could always use my art. Little did I know that I would be making collages for over ten years in outpatient therapy with Dr. Jim. It was through collages that I would come to reconcile my feelings about sexual abuse, finally be able to say goodbye to Paul years later and, eventually, even come to see my mother as a human being.

Another beneficial group at Meadows was psychodrama. It was a catalyst for discovering feelings, both for me and the alters. This group reacquainted me with some long-buried emotions. I would eventually learn more about identifying and tolerating these emotions later in my cognitive therapy group. But before psychodrama, I didn't even know I had emotions—that's what it means to be a stone statue, having no feelings.

I had no idea what psychodrama was, but Dr. Jim had recommended it. I soon learned it involved acting out experiences from your life in a sort of play. Various members of the group would play the part of other people in your life.

The very notion of this made me anxious, but I decided to give it a try.

When I volunteered to reenact a scene from my life, I chose the memory of my mother yelling at me in the morning, "Good girls don't sleep with their fathers!"

I explained what my mother was like to the group member who would play her role. This woman portrayed my mother *so* accurately that I panicked. I froze and couldn't respond to the accusations from "my mother." I was plagued by guilt, feeling all over again how being sexually abused was my fault, feeling I was bad and needed to be punished.

Then, one of the other group members started to cry, inconsolably. As I was frozen, unable to respond or even continue the role-playing exercise, the group turned its attention to the woman who was crying.

Between sobs, she said how terribly sad she felt for me. She was so upset about what happened to the little girl who was coerced into sleeping with her dad and then blamed for it.

Still crying, she came over to hug me and said she was so sorry that I had to go through that.

"Your mother had no right to blame an innocent little girl," she said.

I was shocked! First, *I* had never cried about this incident. I'd never known it was something to cry *about* in the first place. Secondly, the idea that someone could actually blame my mother instead of me was a completely alien thought.

These thoughts struck me like lightening while the woman was hugging me, and I began to cry too.

For the first time, I felt something other than fear when thinking about what had happened to me.

The entire experience was exhausting. I was completely drained afterward and went to my room to lie down.

My mind struggled to understand what had just happened. No one I had ever tried to talk to had responded like this. The police, priests and nuns from my childhood hadn't even *believed* me when I talked to them.

When I had my session with Dr. Jim later that day, I related the experience.

He asked me, "What do you think all of this means?"

It was all so confusing that I had a really hard time answering. But as we talked, I began to admit to myself that maybe I wasn't as bad as my mother made me out to be. At this point, I still hadn't, still couldn't, give up the identity of being inherently bad, but I knew the crying, the feeling of sadness, was genuine.

I finally said, "It *was* sad for a little girl to be blamed for that."

But I couldn't accept the implications of that statement.

Dr. Jim told me it was okay that I was confused and that, for now, learning to be able to feel sad was enough. Psychodrama had sown the seeds for my very first feelings of compassion for myself and the alters. It had also set the stage for future therapy that would ultimately change my entire ideology and beliefs about myself.

It was an odd coincidence that I was in psychodrama just when I needed it. Meadows Hospital discontinued the group shortly after I was discharged.

* * * * *

My homelife during this period of hospitalizations and meeting the alters was chaotic to say the least. I was sometimes co-conscious with the alters and sometimes not.

Ronnie, Jenny, and all the others met and interacted with my husband. At times, this seemed to go well, but not when they were bent on self-destruction. Ronnie sometimes ran away from home and I would find myself at a payphone paging Dr. Jim, not knowing how I'd gotten there. Jenny tried to hurt herself with a coat hanger from the closet a few times. Once, Jenny cut my foot with a razor blade at home. We paged Dr. Norm and he told us my husband would have to take me to the E.R. We were there until after midnight. It was a strain on our marriage.

We didn't understand at the time that all of the alters' actions and behaviors were intended to help me. They all believed that self-punishment and suicide was the only recourse for being so *bad*. They were all trying to prevent worse punishments from my mother, and they believed that if they punished themselves first, it would prevent a world tragedy—a house burning down, a plane crash, a bombing—from occurring. They were punishing themselves first so no one else would have to suffer.

My husband tried hard to help, but this was a lot to cope with. Our biggest fight happened when we were both under a great deal of stress—from hospitalizations, flashbacks, and the fact that I constantly kept switching into alter personalities who were all trying to kill me.

He yelled at me, "Go to hell!"

I know today that he didn't mean it literally, but at the time, that was something I couldn't cope with. I was already in a fragile state, and the word 'hell' threw me into a panic because of my mother's preoccupation with candles and how she always told me I would live forever with Satan.

I flew out of the house and slammed the door, my purse and car keys in hand.

But where would I go?

I drove around the neighborhood crying, and ended up in a parking lot with a payphone. I needed somewhere to go—I *couldn't* go back home.

I had my pocket address book with me, and I flipped through it. I came upon the name of a nurse, Betty, who I worked with at the hospital. She didn't live too far away.... Dare I call her? It was 10 p.m. Apprehensively, I dialed the number. What if she wasn't even home?

She answered, and I told her vaguely about the argument with my husband, and asked if I could come over. Betty was more than supportive, and even offered that I could spend the night.

I needed that reprieve!

When I arrived at Betty's house, I called Dr. Jim and asked him to call my house to let my son know I was okay and that I'd be home in the morning. Even though I couldn't talk to my husband, I knew my son would be worried, and he needed to know I would definitely be coming back.

My husband and I did have other arguments, mostly when I was really stressed out from the intensive therapy but, as time went on, I realized that he was doing the best he could, and truly was trying to be supportive.

Occasionally, when I was in the hospital, we would have family therapy sessions including my husband and Dr. Jim. During these sessions, I explained that I'd been sexually abused by my dad.

Mark was more than willing to try to bring me out of flashbacks by reminding me there was no "brown blanket" on my bed at home and that I was now in the present with a "blue blanket." Mark would point out the differences between my childhood home and our home today. And, although this definitely helped with my memories of Dad, I could not bring myself to tell Mark about my mother's psychotic abuse.

The problem was, I still believed I was evil, as my mother told me, and I didn't want Mark to find out what a horrible person he was married to. I also believed that if I revealed secrets about my mother to Mark, she would find out—either through the "Little People" or through magic—and make something terrible happen to him.

And then, of course, it would be my fault—just another bad thing to feel guilty and suicidal about.

THE WORK I'D BEGUN AT Meadows Hospital in the psychodrama group continued in the form of an out-patient cognitive therapy group.

A psychiatrist on staff at Meadows, Dr. Alan, led our weekly meetings. The most important thing I learned from him was how to recognize and accept emotion.

He began each session by going around the room and asking each of us to share two feelings we'd had that day.

This was very difficult for me. *Stone statues don't have any feelings.* I have to come up with *two?*

I had problems accepting that a person could have more than one feeling at a time. To me everything was either-or, black and white.

Dr. Alan said if we had a hard time identifying an emotion, we should listen to our body. "Sometimes that can help clue you in. The connection between emotions in your head and physical feelings in your body can be an advantage," he said.

An *advantage?* That was a difficult concept for me to wrap my mind around. Feeling like I had to urinate had so enraged my mother that I'd learned from a very young age to deny any and all physical sensations. I had also taught myself to become numb to physical pain after enduring so many beatings. I knew the beatings would only be worse if I cried out, or showed her the leather strap hurt in any way.

But since Dr. Jim and I had discussed the importance of separating the past from the present, I decided to give Dr. Alan's new concept a try.

Physical sensations were really foreign to me, but with practice, I began to become aware of them again.

Learning to pay attention went slowly for me. But Dr. Alan had a "Feelings Chart" on the wall, which helped. The chart had pictures of facial expressions and corresponding emotions written beneath each one. I frequently stood up and walked over to that chart to help me identify a feeling.

With time, I soon learned Dr. Alan was right. Amazingly, just as he predicted, there were different physical sensations connected to every emotion. For me, anger showed up as a tightness in my neck and shoulders. Fear showed up as a tightening of my chest.

I became more and more proficient at this process. I learned to ask myself questions when a physical sensation arose. For example, if I noticed my neck hurting, I'd ask myself, "Is there anything that happened recently that I might be angry about?"

Dr. Alan's technique which was at first so alien, became my map for navigating this new, confusing world of emotions.

Dr. Alan taught us other cognitive therapy techniques, too.

I learned to do a cost-benefit analysis of issues such as changing my beliefs, questioning the validity of suicidal thoughts, and running away.

I learned there were some benefits to holding onto my belief that *I am bad*. And there were both advantages and disadvantages to changing that belief. The cost-benefit approach helped me learn how to rationally weigh the pros and cons of every decision.

I discovered that most of my reasons for wanting to hold onto the belief that *I am evil* stemmed from fear—both of my mother and of the unknown.

Tackling the latter proved especially challenging. I had absolutely *no* framework for viewing myself as anything other than an inherently bad person.

Dr. Jim and I spent many sessions discussing how life could and would be different by changing my self-concept. It was terrifying.

Believing *I am evil* gave me a feeling of control: It offered a reason, an explanation, for everything that happened in the world—from early childhood abuse to the Oklahoma City Bombing.

I was frightened to enter into a world of uncertainty.

In order to make that leap, I needed to be able to separate *me* from the abuse, and *me* from *I'm evil* and *I'm the reason bad things happen*.

I slowly learned that an individual is separate from the events that happen in his or her life. An individual has feelings and can "own" them without succumbing to outside influences.

Dr. Jim taught me to recognize what I feel on the inside and to learn to hold on to that *in spite of* what anyone else says. This concept took many individual sessions with Dr. Jim—as well as many group sessions with Dr. Alan—to practice. But it was worth the struggle.

I still wasn't convinced I was not evil, but learning these cognitive strategies was crucial to eventually being able to counter that belief.

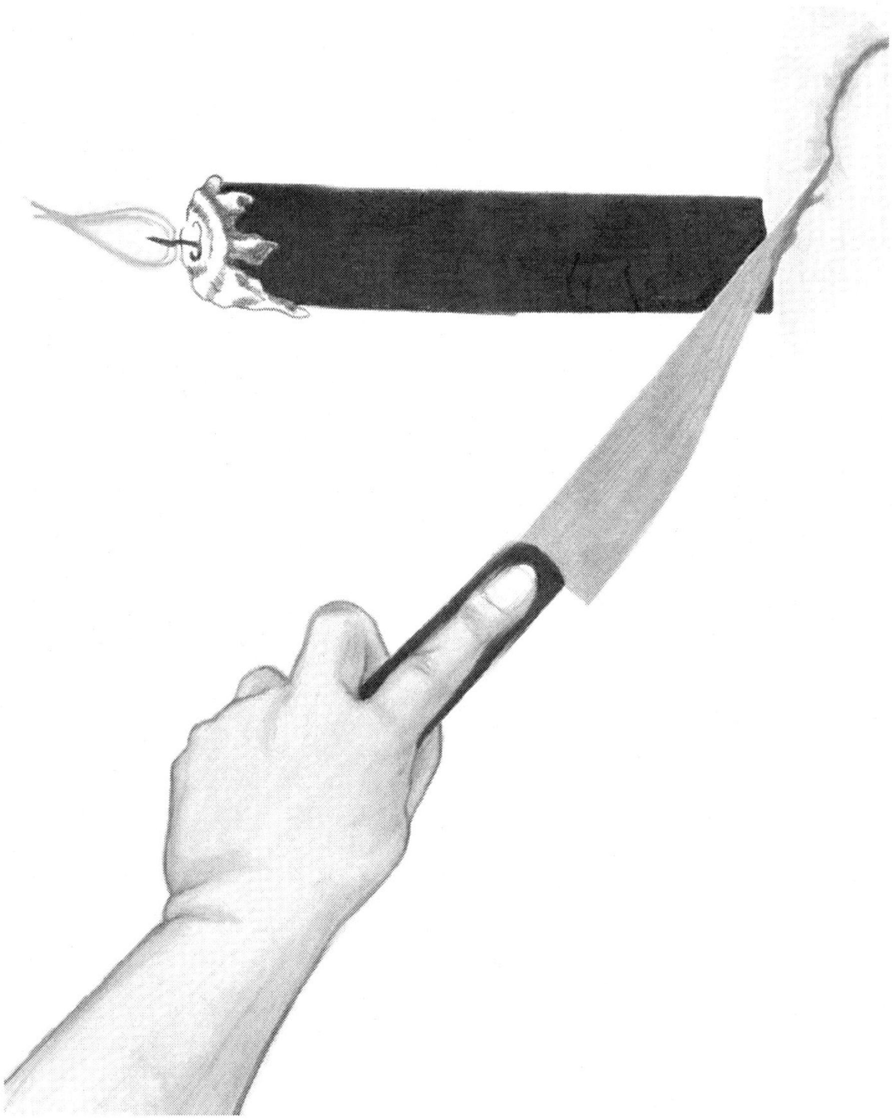

JOYCE WAS A PATIENT IN the cognitive therapy group with me.

When I first met her, I never would have believed it possible that she would become my first real friend. The Second and Third Amendments made friendship illegal.

But Joyce was persistent. At first, one evening when the group was over, she approached me and said, "You know, I've always wanted a friend like you."

I panicked. Talking to people in group was one thing, but extending it beyond the group was a crime punishable by death.

I told her several times, "No, I don't give out my phone number."

I can't tell you how scared I was.

But Joyce was never pushy, and she let me come around in my own time. Finally, months later, I agreed to go over to her apartment after group. She only lived a few blocks away.

It was during the holiday season, and I didn't know she had invited someone else from the group as well.

When we arrived at Joyce's apartment, the other woman asked me, "Where are your things?"

I had no clue what she was talking about. Apparently, when friends get together for dinner around Christmas, each person brings a dish and gifts for everyone. As I had no experience with friends, I didn't bring anything. It was awkward and embarrassing to say the least.

But they didn't say anything about it, and tried not to make me feel bad or uncomfortable. Actually, I was shocked that these women apparently cared enough about me that they each gave me a present. (Wasn't I a bad, terrible, evil person?) One of the gifts, which I still cherish today, was a golden star ornament that Joyce handmade for me. I never knew she was really into making crafts.

After that night, I still had a hard time talking to her—this was all so new to me—but we began arriving for group early and would talk in the parking lot.

Oh, I still thought about sabotaging our friendship, and I was paranoid that something terrible would befall her as punishment for being my friend. I was concerned about her health; I worried she would die in a car crash; I imagined my mother's wrath if the "Little People" told her about Joyce.

After several years of being in the group, Joyce announced she was getting married—a big step for her. She had also just finished her degree at school. She truly was making progress in her therapy. She'd even become a role model for me.

Shortly after that, Joyce moved out of state with her new husband to be closer to her in-laws. For me, this was both good and bad. In a way, I was glad because it lessened my burden of worrying about her safety. I reasoned that the further away from me she was, the safer she'd be.

On the other hand, I was sad to see her go. This was the first friendship I'd made in my life that I hadn't sabotaged. Joyce and I continued a "long-distance friendship," calling each other on the phone to share our ups and downs. If either of us had a crisis, we knew the other was just a phone call away. We'd even make those "safety contracts" with each other over the phone whenever either of us was in "self-harm mode."

It's been years since I've seen her, but we still send each other gifts around the holidays, and I can always count on Joyce to send me a new teddy bear on Christmas.

. . . . . .

EVEN THOUGH I WAS LEARNING about having and accepting feelings, I never knew a person was capable of crying as many tears as I did during those years.

I distinctly remember sitting on my bed in the hospital one day asking Dr. Jim, "If I have to have feelings, why do they all have to be bad?"

There was no way for me to know that years from then, I would discover joy.

Right now, I was going through hell.

I cried every day—for myself, and for Ronnie.

Ronnie was the gateway to a whole other world of existence, and a further realization of my mother's psychotic behavior. Through Ronnie, I learned of Mother's involvement in the occult.

I already knew that she was obsessed with candles and that, on many occasions, she tried to control me, saying, "I'll light a candle on you if you don't behave."

Ronnie told us mother and a group of friends were involved with candles and magic. My mother had been taking Ronnie to their meetings.

Ronnie was told that on her seventh birthday, she would have to light a candle, admit she was evil, and follow these peoples' beliefs and practices.

This explained why she insisted on remaining six years old for the rest of her life.

We learned that two other alters, Jenny and Jennifer, took over for Ronnie so that she could remain six.

Jennifer had no feelings, and thus no fear, so she performed many tasks that were too scary for Ronnie.

Jenny, meanwhile, lit the candle that Ronnie refused to on her seventh birthday. When Jenny took over, she was forced to walk in line with Mother's friends, carrying a candle under the threat of punishment, and Mother made her repeat, over and over again out loud that she was evil and that she was going to hell.

To Jenny, it didn't matter that she was obeying Mother only under the threat of punishment. The fact that she was participating in this ritual, regardless of the reason, solidified in her mind that she *was* evil.

She In Perspective

When Jenny recounted these memories in Dr. Jim's office, we helped her by giving her an "alternate ending" to the memory. Dr. Jim let her retrace her steps, thereby retracting the footsteps she had taken so many years ago.

And she pictured me, Jody, the adult, walking with her and holding her hand to keep her safe. This formula of having me, as the adult, accompanying the child alters would, after years of therapy, finally allay their fears.

But for the moment, we all remained convinced we were evil.

That was the worst part, for all of us, all the alters—Mother's relentless mantra. *You're a bad girl! All the bad things in the world happen because of you!*

Ronnie was convinced it was true when she refused to carry the candle in the ritual that marked her seventh birthday.

It was a no-win scenario for all of us. Jenny, who took over for Ronnie, was convinced she was evil for taking part in the ritual. Ronnie was convinced she was bad for disobeying Mother by not taking part in the ritual.

We were all convinced that no matter what we did, it was wrong, that we were bad and, because of that, Mother was going to cause some horrible tragedy to occur, either to us or to someone we loved.

During this intense therapy with Ronnie, I became obsessed with candles in the present. The terror of the memories was so real to Ronnie that it became hard to distinguish the past from the present, and I found myself performing "candle rituals" before every therapy session with Dr. Jim.

I bought some candles and took them with me every time I drove to go see Dr. Jim. About a half mile from his office, I would park in a remote area of a shopping center. There, I got out of the car, sat on the pavement, and lit the candles. As they were burning, I let the hot wax drip over my hands. This, I felt, would punish both me and Ronnie for not obeying my mother. I hoped that this self-punishment would stave of her anger, prevent her from coming to get us, and prove that we understood how evil we really were. This candle ritual continued for months.

I went through psychotic episodes when the flashbacks of sadistic abuse frequently seemed more real than the present day. Dealing with all these memories was as much as I could handle at that time and I finally became unable to go on functioning as a "normal" person on a day-to-day basis.

During one hospitalization, Dr. Jim said he felt I was not stable enough to return to work and thought it best for me to go on disability.

This in itself was traumatizing. There were questionnaires to fill out; numerous psychiatric interviews; I had to talk about triggers, alters, flashbacks, and on and on.

One of the hardest parts of applying for disability was that the psychiatric interviews had to be conducted downtown. Talk about a trigger. I hadn't been

Memories on the Wall

downtown for many years, and as soon as I saw those tall buildings, I was immediately absorbed by a flashback.

I relived being raped when I was 13. This time, I finally remembered the circumstances surrounding that day. Another patient and I had managed to escape from D at the state psychiatric hospital. This girl had told me that if we managed to get away, she knew some guys we could stay with downtown. But we paid the price.

I don't think I'd been back downtown since. Now, standing outside the interview building, I cried and cried. I couldn't stop crying throughout my interview. Fortunately, the psychiatrist was sympathetic, and my husband, supportive.

Six months later I began receiving disability checks.

BEING ON DISABILITY ALLOWED ME to devote most of my time to therapy.

One of the (many) issues I was working through now was being blamed when our neighbor's house burned down.

I remember standing outside beside my mother, watching the firemen battling the blaze. "If only you could behave, this fire never would have started!" she said.

I tried and tried for years to figure out what I'd done wrong, but just couldn't understand. The only possible conclusion, I thought, was that I was just born bad, and that nothing I did or tried to do would ever change that.

Over and over again, I was blamed for everything bad in the world.

This mindset was so ingrained that when the Oklahoma City Bombing happened in 1995, I was one hundred percent certain that I had caused it *and* that I should die for causing all those innocent people to lose their lives.

I was so suicidal that I was hospitalized for a month. I repeated this same pattern over and over. A car accident or a plane crash that I heard about on the news—I was convinced that all of these things were my fault and that I should die.

Dr. Norm and I nicknamed these episodes Back Words. Dr. Norm originally coined the term when he saw me playing the boardgame called *Back Words* with Don in the ICU at Meadows. The object is to rearrange any letters already on the board into new words.

The word 'live' was on the board when Dr. Norm observed that my mother's messages were exactly like the game. He rearranged the letters to spell 'evil.'

"'Live' is 'evil' spelled backwards," Dr. Norm explained. "Your mother's messages are backward explanations of the way things really are in life."

So, when I would call him in a crisis, all I had to say was, "It's the Back Words thing again."

All of the memories from all of the alters had one thing in common—the same haunting vision of my mother's face, with those angry eyes, and I knew I *had* to be punished or else some world catastrophe would occur.

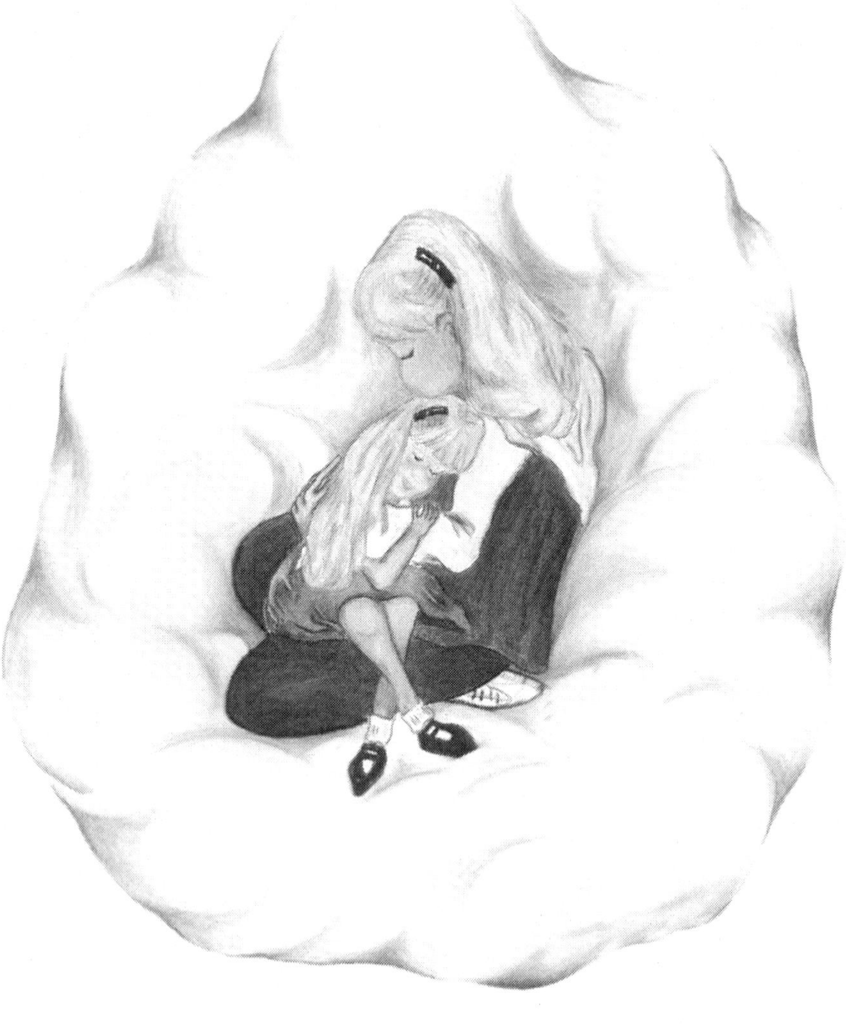

Similar to lighting candles in the parking lot, I developed a ritual in adulthood to punish myself and "appease" my mother.

It was the old habit of cutting myself with razor blades—with a twist. I would cut myself repeatedly and collect the blood in a medicine cup. I reasoned that if I could bleed enough, if I could collect enough blood, I could prove to my mother and to myself that my punishment was adequate.

Cutting myself in adulthood served dual purposes. First, it was a convenient means of punishing myself for being evil, since I no longer had my mother to do it.

It was also a way to relieve the pain brought on by childhood memories. It would take many years of therapy before I would finally be able to break the habit of cutting myself as a means to those ends.

During the years I was a cutter and contemplating suicide, those years of streaming, unrelenting memories, I spent many days in intensive care at the hospital, often in seclusion and restraints. I was so insistent that I needed to die that those were the only means the staff had to protect me from myself.

But I became a master at getting *out* of restraints. One time, I succeeded in getting free only to tie one of the leather restraint straps around my neck. I was turning blue by the time the nurses discovered what I was doing.

My doctors frequently adjusted my medications to control depression, my switching between personalities, my memories, and my self-destructive behaviors.

I was tried on Elavil, Prozac, Paxil, Lamictal, Lithium, Risperdal, Zyprexa, Tenex, Clonidine, Ativan, and Geodon, (not to mention Thorazine and Haldol when I was 13).

At one point, I was up to a daily dose of 100mg of Zyprex on an as needed basis. The recommended maximum dose is 20mg. Nevertheless, Dr. Jim and Dr. Norm had faith in me and stuck with me through it all.

It was October of 1994.

And again, like every October I could remember, I was becoming anxious. This year was even worse. One of my worst memories was coming back to haunt me. I needed to know what really happened to Paul.

Up until now, Ronnie had only remembered attending his funeral. We were about to learn the truth.

Ronnie began the story. It was Halloween night, and we were five years old.

Ronnie went with my mother to Paul's house, but she knew something was wrong the minute she walked through the door.

The house was lit only by candlelight. All of Mother's friends were already there, waiting for us.

The adults told Ronnie to kiss Paul for the last time.

Paul had always been a rebel, and never liked to do what the adults told him to. In that respect, Paul and Ronnie were alike, and that's why they were such close friends.

I guess the only difference was that I had alters, and there was no option for Paul.

My mother told Ronnie plainly, "Paul's going to die tonight. He needs to learn his lesson, and so do you. So do all children who don't do as they're told."

The adults held my hand (but not *my hand*) and made me (but *not me*, and *not* Ronnie) hold Paul's head under water in the bathtub.

None of us could do that to our friend!

She did it. From that moment on, She was the only alter who remembered all the horrible details of that night. She felt totally responsible for Paul's death.

Even though I didn't remember it, what had happened continued to haunt me every Halloween for the next 40 years.

It was an eerie experience when She finally recounted the events in Dr. Jim's office. I could feel Paul's presence in the room. Now that She said it aloud, Ronnie, Jenny, and everyone else knew what had happened. And I knew. And Dr. Jim knew.

I also knew I had to be put to death for killing our friend, Paul.

For years after the telling of it, I'd become extremely suicidal around Halloween, knowing I had to kill myself before October 31.

Dr. Norm and Dr. Jim knew they had to work overtime with me every fall. I took extra medication and made safety contracts. But I still blamed myself for Paul's death.

My first memory of Paul had resurfaced in 1993. It wouldn't be until 2007 that I'd finally come to terms with losing him, and place the blame where it belonged, realizing a five-year-old girl could *not* possibly be responsible.

To this day, I don't know if the drowning was real or was simply staged. I don't know if Paul lived or not. All I know is that my mother told me I killed Paul, and I believed her. After that dreadful night in 1963, Paul's family moved away. All that mattered to me was that he was gone and I was to blame.

In addition to my fear of certain days of the year, such as Halloween, I learned that Ronnie was afraid of nights when there was either a full moon or when the stars were aligned to the left of the moon to form an arrow in the sky.

My mother had told Ronnie that if she didn't light candles on those nights to atone for all her bad behavior, she would be the cause of someone's death.

After I recovered the memories Ronnie held for so long—memories that I had denied—I, too, became deathly afraid of seeing the moon and the stars.

I didn't want to cause anything else to happen to anyone!

I talked about this fear of the moon and the stars at great length with Dr. Norm and Dr. Jim. Dr. Norm suggested that I do a homework project on Selenology—a scientific study of the moon—to learn what the moon actually is.

But the very thought of it frightened me even more, sending me into a panic for weeks. Studying the moon meant challenging what Mother said about it. I didn't dare defy her like that.

The only thing that could calm me down was *not* thinking about the moon or the stars at all. For quite some time, that meant never going outside after sunset.

I didn't revisit the issue again for many months.

When I did, Dr. Jim told me to try to think logically about the moon. He pointed out that I had not lit any candles during the full moon for a long time, and asked me, "Has anyone you know ever died when there was a full moon?"

"No."

He pointed out that during all of the years I denied my memories I had not lit any candles. So, if what my mother told Ronnie was true, then every month for the past 15 years, there would have been tragedies on those days.

I realized he was right, but the thought of the moon still made me anxious. I was able to see the logic of what he was saying, but this was all part of the "magical thinking" I wasn't able to give up, not yet.

Later in therapy, Dr. Jim and I would use cognitive therapy to dispel the magic, once and for all.

* * * * * *

During the two years I was on disability, therapy was unrelenting, but Dr. Jim and I both felt I was making progress.

I was seeing Dr. Jim usually twice a week, and attending my survivors' group on Monday evenings. My husband and I were also going to marriage counseling every other week.

Then, I became pregnant.

My husband and I hadn't engaged in sex for quite a while, as it triggered flashbacks of my father. I always saw the brown blanket on his bed.

But, with all the intensive therapy, apprehensively, I decided to give sex a try and got pregnant.

I did *not* need that kind of stress! I was on a plethora of psychiatric medications, all of which were dangerous to a pregnancy. For that reason, my doctors all recommended having an abortion.

They also felt that given my fragile emotional state, I would not be capable of caring for a newborn.

I vacillated morning and night, day after day. I cried daily, hourly.

After several weeks, I started bleeding. I called the obstetrician immediately and was seen at the hospital. They performed a vaginal ultrasound which showed that part of the placenta had separated.

I knew it must have been my fault. I must have done something wrong! The doctor was surprised at the findings—he thought I'd had a miscarriage. But the fetus was still alive, which only made my indecisiveness worse. All of my doctors continued to recommend having an abortion. They felt the problem was due to all my medication and that there was little chance of the baby surviving.

I had an abortion at seven weeks.

As fate would have it, my abortion coincided with the Oklahoma City Bombing.

I went into a psychotic state.

I was absolutely, proof-positive, certain-sure that the Oklahoma City Bombing was caused by my choosing to have an abortion.

All those people had died because of the way I killed my child. I had no choice but to kill myself for being the cause of all those people in Oklahoma losing their lives.

Dr. Norm hospitalized me for a month.

That hospital stay was one of the hardest I endured. I stayed in intensive care the entire time. Every day, I told the staff I was the worst person on the planet.

Even under close supervision, I still found ways to harm myself, with the alters' help. The only time I was alone was in the bathroom. That's when Jenny came to my aid. She took over and removed the cardboard insert from the toilet paper and jammed it completely up into my vagina. She thought that was the only way to permanently harm us so that we could never again have a baby to kill. Punishment was the only recourse for what we had done.

When the staff discovered what I did to myself, I was placed in restraints. But I broke free and tied the bed sheets together to hang myself.

From self-harm to suicide, it was one attempt after another. My mother's lessons were deeply ingrained: I needed to be punished for all the horrible things I caused.

After a month of intensive therapy, I was only just beginning to understand what the staff and my doctors were trying to tell me: there is no magical connection between me, my life circumstances, and "world tragedies," as I called them.

I began to concede that *maybe* I didn't cause the bombing, but I still could not turn off the old messages that *I was evil*.

I was finally discharged with the stipulation that I would sign a "No Harm Contract" with both Dr. Jim and Dr. Norm.

Throughout all of my hospitalizations, Dr. Norm always said, "Think of memories as just pictures on the wall. You can look at them, but then you can just walk past them."

I tried *so hard*, but the past still haunted me.

BETWEEN HOSPITALIZATIONS, I WAS HAVING more difficulties at home. I began getting extremely paranoid. I would double lock all the doors in the house, certain that my mother, her friends, or those "Little People" would find me. I was having too many memories to feel safe anywhere.

One day at the gas station, I was sure the attendants were watching me and would follow me. I was sure that *someone*, then *everyone* I saw, was after me. They were all going to punish me or hurt me in some way for being such an *evil person*.

By now I had revealed too many family secrets—to Dr. Jim, to Dr. Norm, the hospital staff, and to the members of the outpatient groups.

It was cemented in my brain that talking about things is *wrong*. I wasn't afraid of being locked in the garage for talking as I had been as a child, but, somehow, somewhere, my mother would be "lighting candles on me" to make something bad happen to me, or because of me.

I was so brainwashed by her that there was no doubt in my mind.

For years, I couldn't watch the news. Every car crash, every accident they reported—everything was my fault. I could always come up with some way to connect these things back to me. One day at home, I was doing a journaling assignment from Dr. Jim about the anger I felt towards my mother. When I needed a break, I drove to the grocery store.

There, in the parking lot, I watched in shock as an elderly man lost control of his car and crashed into a bank. It was my fault! I never should have written that I was angry with my mother! I wasn't behaving right, again! My mother was sending me a message through the car crash. I had to kill myself.

The pattern continued. Dr. Jim and Dr. Norm tried to explain that there is no magic. These things were all coincidences.

I wasn't ready to accept any of it.

It was one trigger after another.

In 1995, my son was in eighth grade at a Catholic school and was getting confirmed in church.

The candles all around the church triggered memories of my mother and her rituals. I panicked. What would happen to me? Would something bad happen to me ... or to my son?

Fortunately, my husband was sensitive to my triggers and had suggested I bring a teddy bear with me in my purse.

I also brought my small wind-up toy from Dr. Jim's office with me. Through-

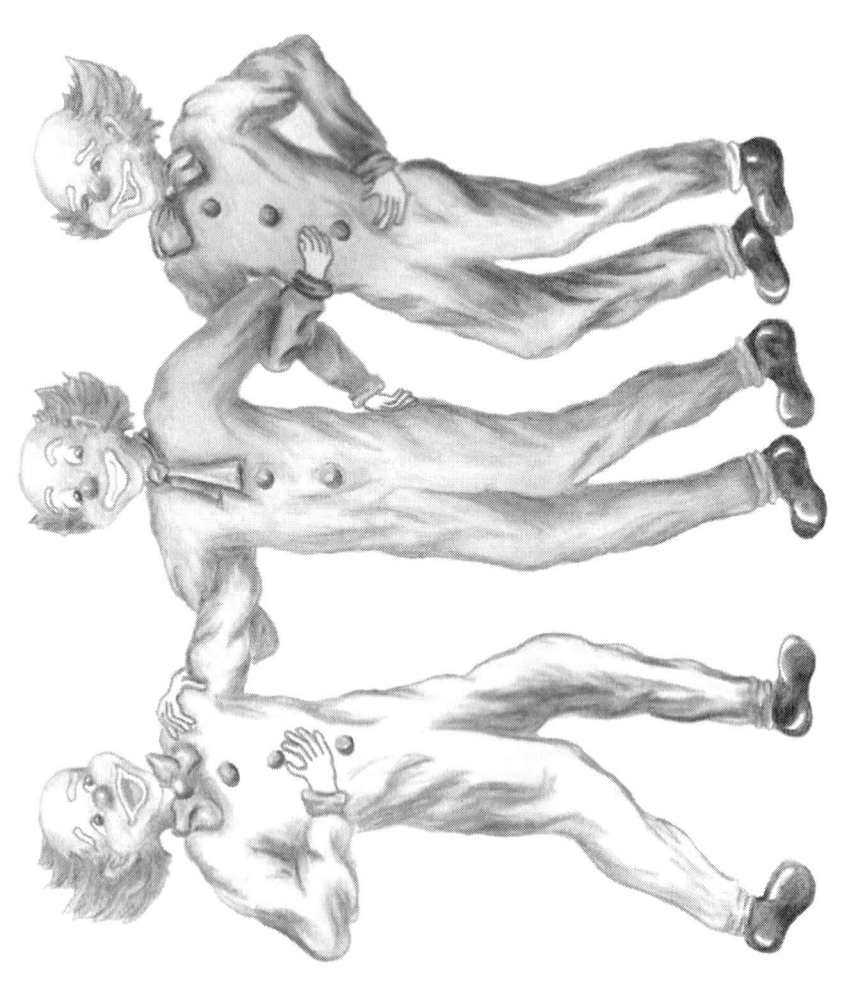

The alters after therapy—"Friends on the Inside"

out the ceremony, I held these toys while visualizing the safe room in my mind that Dr. Jim and I had come up with. Using these strategies was the only way to survive the confirmation ceremony.

Although I made it through this particular event, most of my time on disability, when the alters were sharing their stories, their fears and feelings, we were all out of control.

I was switching between personalities erratically, and we were always self destructive. I carried a razor blade with me in my purse at all times during those years, "just in case I needed one."

One day, in Dr. Jim's waiting room, Jenny took over. She took out the razor blade, cut my arm, and wrote Dr. Jim a message on a piece of paper—in blood.

Dr. Jim called 911. When the ambulance arrived, they put me on a stretcher, and tied me down.

Dr. Jim said, "I know you can't control anything right now. This is for the best."

I was taken to intensive care at the hospital, where I remained in restraints.

The alters were all trying to take over simultaneously. One after another.

I truly felt I was going crazy.

Finally, Dr. Jim came to the unit. He said, "I want to talk to everyone. I want all of you to listen. It won't help for all of you to try to talk at once. I know you are all upset, but Jody needs to rest now. And for her to be able to help you, you all need to relax and take a break. I want you each to promise to take turns. Everyone will get their turn to talk. But right now, Jody and all of you need to rest. Can you promise me that? And then we'll help."

And then the voices were quiet. I was let out of restraints 15 minutes later.

It took months and months of hearing all the alters' stories before, very slowly, they came to trust Dr. Jim first, and then, to trust me. With trust began the healing.

My first real breakthrough with an alter came when Ronnie felt enough trust in Dr. Jim and in me that she was able to overcome her fear of turning seven and have a safe birthday.

Ronnie always said, "I don't like numbers." But after months and months of explaining to her, through words and through drawings, that there are no bad or scary people anymore, that my mother is not here and couldn't hurt her anymore or make her do anything she didn't want to do, she agreed to have a birthday.

We threw her a party, complete with a chocolate cake with the number seven on it, in Dr. Jim's office. My husband was there, as well as Dr. Jim and his partner, Dr. Susan.

This in and of itself was a breakthrough for Ronnie, as she had been terrified of adult women. Ronnie even asked Dr. Susan to light the candles.

After that day, Ronnie became my number-one ally in working with the other alters. The fact that nothing bad happened when Ronnie turned seven was a solid piece of evidence that the bad people, my parents and my mother's friends, were indeed gone.

And Ronnie was living proof, to me and the other alters, that fear could indeed be conquered.

The hardest and most time-consuming part of therapy was not the memories themselves, but convincing myself and the alters that whenever bad things happened, it was not our fault.

My parents' old tapes of guilt and blame played over and over, and I believed it all with every part of my mind.

Every alter believed it.

Even "The Little One," who was a toddler that mother terrorized by threatening to burn alive on the stove, believed he was *bad*.

His vocabulary only consisted of a few words. So he would just sit in a corner and cringe, thinking he was bad and deserved Mother's abuse.

Jenny and Jennifer knew they were bad because they lit candles like my mother told them to. They believed the act of lighting the candles demonstrated that they *wanted* bad things to happen. Jenny and Jennifer were created to go along with my mother's psychotic rituals when I, Ronnie, and Little Jody could not.

Little Jody knew we were all bad because she watched the sexual acts with dad and knew what happened was wrong. She heard, every time I did, when my mother yelled, "Good girls don't sleep with their fathers!" Sometimes Little Jody took the beatings in my place. She lived her life in shame.

Janet was in limbo at 17. She remained suicidal and never turned 18 because she believed the only way to cope with a life that was intolerable was to die.

And those were only the alters we'd met so far.

* * * * * *

MEETING JEFF WAS THE NEXT major crisis.

Dr. Jim and I were talking about how much I missed Dad when I suddenly switched into an alter personality we had never met before.

I was not co-conscious, and only became aware of the events that transpired after we integrated. At the time, all I knew was that our session began and, a moment later, it was over.

Dr. Jim was aware of the switch and somehow got Jeff to introduce himself. He was a 13-year-old boy who came into being when Dad abandoned me.

Completely devastated and with no one to turn to, I'd needed to find some way to still be able to relate to dad. I did that by becoming a boy. The strategy apparently succeeded somewhat, as Dad and Jeff did "guy things" together—they worked on cars and built things.

Finally, at least in some capacity, I had Dad back—although as Jody, I was unaware of it.

Dr. Jim formed an alliance with Jeff by showing him the toolbox that he kept in his office closet. They became buddies.

The crisis occurred when Dr. Jim and I tried to bring Jeff into the present—to show him what year it was, and how things had changed.

Dr. Jim and I developed the concept of an inside clock and an outside clock to help explain this to the alters. I made a colorful crayon drawing of two clocks, and we explained that time always goes by on the outside clock, but sometimes, the hands on the inside clock get stuck so you don't realize that any time has passed. It's like being asleep for awhile.

We explained to Jeff that 20 years had passed on the outside while he was sleeping on the inside.

As Jeff started to understand this, he soon came to realize this meant his dad was nowhere to be found. He was scared. He was devastated. His entire world had revolved around Dad.

Jeff lost control. At home, he punched walls and kicked furniture, breaking the bones in my right foot. (That was kind of hard to explain to the medical doctor and X-ray technicians.) Jeff was so self-destructive that I agreed to be hospitalized again.

What happened that time at Meadows was unbelievable.

Dr. Jim thought the hospital would be the safest place to explain to Jeff that Dad had passed away. So Dr. Jim and I had a session in one of the small, unoccupied group rooms on the unit. I brought in pictures of Dad, as well a Holy Card from Dad's funeral, to show Jeff.

Jeff became enraged. He took control from me, bolted up, grabbed a chair, and threw it at Dr. Jim.

Dr. Jim ducked and called a "Code 44."

A number of male staff members were finally able to subdue Jeff. He was put in restraints and taken to the intensive care unit where a "One to One" staff member was assigned to watch him. Even with all of these safeguards, he continued to bang our fractured foot against the bed.

Jeff was hospitalized for weeks. He wanted no part of doctors, treatment, safety contracts, medication—nothing. He wanted his dad.

Dr. Norm had an idea. Jeff had told him that the one thing he'd always wanted was a blue boy's bike. So Dr. Norm got Jeff to agree that if he participated in therapy, did his assignments, and stopped hitting and throwing things, he would

The Inside Clock   *The Outside Clock*

When you are on the inside, sleeping, time hands on the inside clock are stuck, so you don't know that any time has passed. For you, it is still 1965.

On the outside, time never pauses, or even slows down. Many years have gone by. It is now 1995

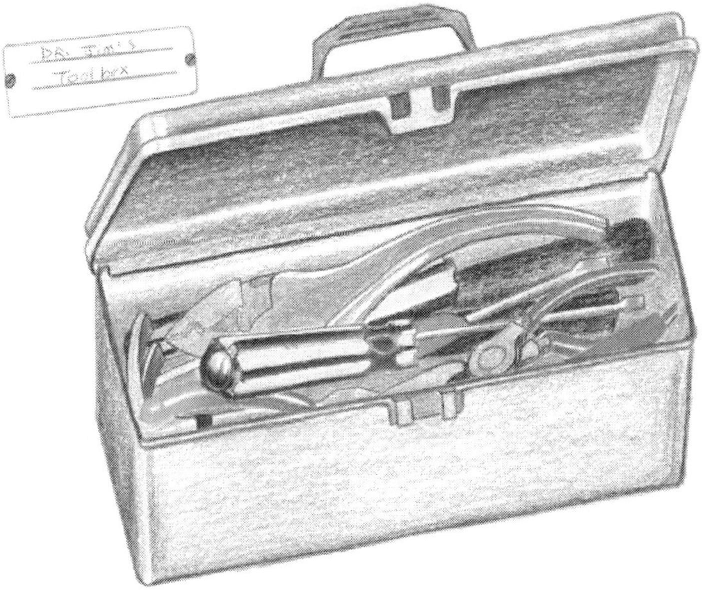
Dr. Jim's
Toolbox

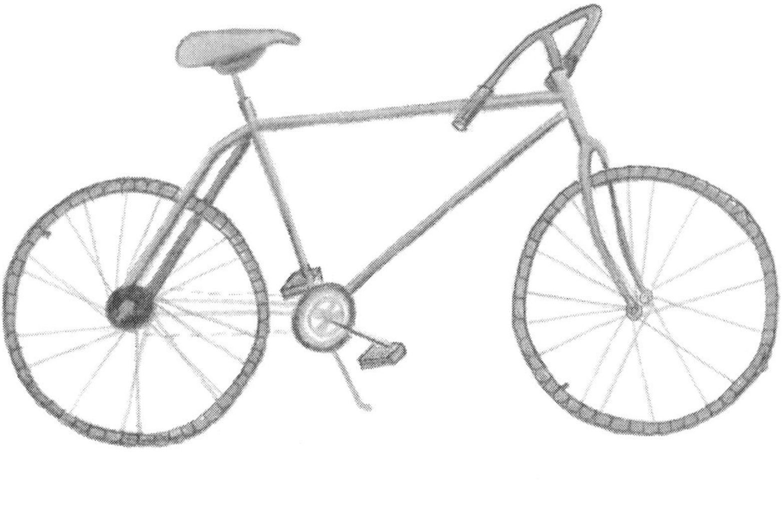

get his blue bike. Dr. Norm found a picture of a bike in a magazine and taped it to the wall in Jeff's room.

Jeff had a lot of anger, a lot of sadness, a lot of grief. But, slowly, he learned to cope. Dr. Norm gave him an anger workbook, and Jeff learned to express his feelings with words instead of through acting out.

It was hit or miss for quite a while but, as a team, we did get Jeff to accept that Dad was gone and that we were here for him.

I gave him his bike in the safe room in my mind.

Jeff and I cried together about missing dad, and only together were we able to say goodbye. That was a milestone for Jeff, and for me as well, since I had never cried at or after Dad's funeral.

Jeff and I integrated easily after that, and, after all these years, I finally had a realistic view of Dad. I was now able to see him as a human being, with both good qualities and bad. Dad must have suffered a lot himself. He had been in a bad marriage and had a lot of his own pain to contend with.

This did not excuse what he did to me, but seeing him as a complete person allowed me to forgive him and thank him for the good things he taught me. He had taught me how to treat people, like the way he respected his friends.

Aside from the abuse, he gave me a strong sense of right and wrong. He taught me to work hard and follow through on what I believed in. He instilled values in me that I still hold dear to this day.

DURING MY FIRST OUTPATIENT APPOINTMENT with Dr. Norm after Jeff and I integrated, I found myself playing with transformers out in the waiting room.

"I've never seen you so *present* before," Dr. Norm said. "You're really here!"

It was a good feeling.

I was too involved in therapy, memories and learning skills to be aware of the outside world. Dr. Norm's observation that I was "really here" was the first objective feedback that told me something was changing.

Other people had also begun noticing the changes I could not yet see.

Dr. Jim's secretary, Marci, saw it, too.

I had been seeing Dr. Jim for years by now and, naturally, talked to his secretary, Marci, on a weekly basis. We would chat while I was in the waiting room—not about the issues I was working through—just small talk. I thought I was in my "actress" mode the entire time. But one day when we were talking, she said to me, "You know, you've really changed. You're a lot less anxious than you used to be."

I was taken aback. First of all, I hadn't realized that I *was* less anxious. Second, I didn't know anyone could see through my "actress" persona.

Dr. Jim and I spent the entire session that day discussing the incident. "That's how it is with change," he said. "Many times others notice it in you before you notice it yourself."

Apparently, releasing all of those long-buried memories and connecting with the alters was actually having an effect on me, but it scared me that Marci had noticed a *change*.

I didn't know who or what I was changing *into*. I was afraid of the unknown.

The incident with Marci was one of my first indications that I was afraid of "getting better." Dr. Jim and I would eventually explore and confront this fear.

But for now, I simply knew I was scared. I also knew, fear or not, I had to keep working with the alters.

As all of the alters recounted their memories, there were two key strategies that helped. We worked hard to give the alters a sense of safety. We also had to help them realize that whatever happened was not their fault.

Essential in cultivating a sense of safety was helping the alters understand that they were in the present, that many years had passed since the events they were remembering, and that there was no longer anyone around who could hurt them.

This is where the concept of the inside clock and the outside clock was really helpful. Although time on their inside clocks had not changed since the 1960s, while they were asleep, the outside clock kept ticking and it was now 1995. I, Jody, had moved to a new house, far away from Mother and Dad.

At first it was difficult for the alters to understand, but as I showed them the house and objects around us in the present, they began to feel safer.

The next challenge was helping the alters realize they were not bad, and no one was blaming or punishing them. This would be essential in order for us to integrate.

To help accomplish this, Dr. Alan, Dr. Jim, and I used several techniques I'd first learned in the cognitive therapy group.

First, we led the alters through a series of questions.

Focusing on one experience at a time, each alter would consider a specific event from the past, and ask:

If I did that, what does that say about me?

If that's true about me, then what does *that mean*?

The question and answer series would continue until the final answer had arrived at a fundamental belief, such as: "I'm a bad person."

This technique helped us understand that the *belief* was more of a problem than the actual event.

Another helpful cognitive therapy technique we used was drawing.

Since most of my alters were kids, I used crayons to draw cartoons of an angry mother or other adults, and then a small, cute, but frightened child. I added birds and animals to my pictures.

Then, in a series of subsequent drawings, the cartoon characters would act out the particular memory we were dealing with.

Watching events play out in a cartoon helped the alters realize that the cute little cartoon character could not be to blame, and that it was wrong of the angry mother character to hurt the child, or make the child do bad things.

One by one, the alters came to understand they were not to blame. It was hard for them to accept how frightening the past was, but with Dr. Alan, Dr. Jim and me by their side, they were slowly able to let go of the past.

Integration of the alters always began with each of them telling their stories, sharing their memories—a daunting first step.

But we had discovered that we no longer needed to fear each other or keep secrets. Even early on in therapy, when Ronnie was my number-one ally, Jenny told Dr. Jim, "I want to *be* Ronnie."

Dr. Jim told her it was not yet time. But later, Ronnie, Jenny and Jennifer did finally integrate into one personality.

The very first alter to integrate was The Little One, as he held but a single memory. It was of my mother trying to burn him on the stove. Like all the alters, he too believed he had earned this punishment for misbehaving.

The Little One integrated only after he understood that no little boy deserved to be burned by his own mother.

She held the worst memory—of Paul's death—and the belief that she was to blame for the terrible tragedy.

After *much* therapeutic work, She saw that it was impossible for a five-year-old girl to be responsible, and was then able integrate with Ronnie and Jenny and Jennifer.

Janet blended easily once we all accepted that suicide was no longer the only option. She had her eighteenth birthday and was no longer frozen in time, in college, in intensive care.

Time, safety, and empathy were the key ingredients in the therapeutic process that allowed us all to integrate.

After years of keeping secrets from one another and denying each other's existence, as I helped convince the alters that they were not bad, they slowly came to trust me. They even came to *like* me. This had a greater impact on my self-concept than almost any other aspect of therapy. The alters accepted me, and I accepted them.

I reached a milestone on the path toward acceptance when I recounted a pivotal experience I had when I was 15.

When I told my story, all the alters were listening.

After 15 years of enduring my mother's abuse, the beatings, the rituals, her twisted logic that always placed the blame on me, that always put me in "no-win" scenarios, I somehow became resolute to succumb to her no more.

Years ago, I had tried everything I could think of not to dry or even *touch* those poisoned dishes. And Ronnie too had clung to the doorway with all her might, refusing to go anywhere with Mother. But for all our bravery, those had been hopeless battles. I'd been much too small to have any hope of physically resisting Mother. Finally, I was big enough to back up all my pent-up courage.

"I will not listen to you anymore," I told Mother definitively when I was 15.

Mother went into a rage, rampaging and screaming and threatening me.

But I stood my ground. And the physical abuse stopped then and there. From that day on, I no longer let her beat me. I refused to light candles. I did not go anywhere with her. I would not listen to a single word she said.

All of the alters were impressed with what I had done, and now, more than just respecting me, they *wanted* to be with me. If I'd had the courage to stand up to my mother, then maybe they could really trust me to keep them safe.

Finally, after so many years of clinging to individual identities, rejecting the idea that we were the same person, shared the same Mother, we were finally becoming one.

The voices in my head were becoming quiet—not because of denial, but because of acceptance.

I had not yet met Jessie.

Part Five

THE BEGINNING OF A NEW LIFE – BACK TO WORK

Chipping Away

Why, Mommy, Why?

AMENDMENT VII — 1998 — 40 YEARS OLD

This amendment was proposed and accepted when Jody had returned to work and was no longer being frequently hospitalized.

We amend our decision not to have feelings—as we have discovered joy in painting, going for walks, etc.

We amend our decision to never tell each other our individual experiences, as it feels good to be friends with each other on the inside.

We amend our decision to "act" in *all* situations, as we have discovered it can actually feel good to be a nurse and help others.

We amend our decision to never ask for help, as our doctors have helped us tremendously.

We agree to accept help—both by talking during therapy and taking medication.

We agree to always and forever hate our mother for the horrible things she did to us.

Since I was becoming familiar with my various miniscule feelings, and since the alters had developed friendships and were integrating, I began making time for and taking an interest in things outside of therapy.

I listened to music. I began walking—through parks and around the neighborhood. I began drawing and doing oil paintings. Although I'd never taken a class, I had liked doing art ever since I drew those doctors as angels at Children's Hospital when I was four.

Now, for the first time in my life, I was feeling something good. At first, I had no word to describe this sensation. It was completely new to me. So I asked Dr. Jim what it was. He said, "You'll know."

I looked it up on Dr. Alan's feeling chart. It was joy!

I had found joy, both in my nature walks and in art! Granted, these were solitary activities, but I felt something good for the first time in my life.

There were still flashbacks and setbacks—panic attacks, and occasional suicidal thoughts—but they were no longer occurring constantly. Maybe there was hope for getting better after all.

I felt hope, yes, but I still wasn't seeing things objectively. I was having some real feelings on the inside, but I still wasn't aware of just how much my "stone statue" was crumbling to the outside world.

Marci and Dr. Norm had been the first to notice but, in time, others started noticing as well.

One weekend, my husband and I decided to go to an estate sale in the neighborhood. After looking around for a short time, Mark found a recliner that he said would fit perfectly upstairs.

We purchased the chair and brought it home. But we had a winding staircase and, try as we might, we could not maneuver the chair up the stairs. It was just too big. We tried again and again to no avail.

I was getting frustrated.

"This is *ridiculous!*" I snapped. "This *thing* is not *going* upstairs!"

We put the chair on the back porch instead, and that's where it lives to this day. That was that, and I didn't think any more about it.

But Mark recounted the entire incident at our next session with Dr. Jim, describing how I had reacted. Mark was very happy with me.

"It's like I was actually talking to a *real* person!" Mark said.

I was shocked! I thought back on it and realized, I *did* get frustrated. What's more, I had expressed that frustration.

Was I really expressing honest feelings? Did I really do that?

I realized it had just happened naturally. All of my hard work with Dr. Jim *must* be paying off. So, not only was there hope of getting better, it appeared I truly *was* getting better.

I HAD PROGRESSED IN THERAPY to a point where I was having good days now.

But for me, getting better was not an easy task. For years, I panicked with every step I took. I was convinced that getting better meant the abuse was going to return. Anytime I took a step forward in therapy, the old messages kicked in, and I began cutting myself and becoming suicidal. I had to prove that I was still sick—it was the only way to stay safe.

It was a rather complicated thought process that led me to that conclusion, but it was all perfectly logical to me.

First of all, I knew that whenever I was sick and in Children's Hospital as a four-year-old, I was safe. My parents were not around, I was not beaten or yelled

I think my premise was not wrong. The brick wall was built to keep outside people from hurting me. What I didn't realize was that behind the brick wall was another protective device, which is made of ice. This igloo is not to keep hurtful people out, but to shield me from the hurt I feel inside. This hurt is caused by believing 'I am bad.' It is a very hot ball of flame.

at, I was not told I was bad, and I did not have to sleep with my father. So, I made a strong, early connection that equated being sick with being safe. Getting better meant leaving the hospital and returning to my parents' house of horrors.

Secondly, as I got better in therapy, I had the distinct impression that I was growing up. That was bad because, as a child, when I started growing up, entering adolescence and beginning my period, my dad abandoned me, leaving me with no refuge, no safe haven. Growing up meant being more vulnerable.

Another reason I wanted to stay sick, was that I had an unconscious fear of losing Dr. Norm. Without fail, I'd have an anxiety attack after every appointment. I was seeing him once a month at that point, and always the next day, I'd wake up in full-blown panic-mode.

I didn't understand why this was happening—especially since, overall, I was doing so much better.

As Dr. Jim and I talked about this, we discovered that "doing so much better" was part of the cause. Now, instead of always talking to Dr. Norm about crises, flashbacks, and suicide, there were also some good things to tell him. And I was unconsciously terrified that if he really knew how much better I was doing, he would say I didn't need to see him any longer. I still saw Dr. Norm as my "savior," just as I had seen the doctors at Children's Hospital when I was four. I associated losing a doctor with having the abuse start all over again. Dr. Jim called it an "emotional flashback."

During our exploration of this problem, our discussions turned to issues of control, choices, and independence. We used the same cognitive strategies that had helped me overcome other issues. Dr. Jim pointed out that, in contrast to what had happened when I was four, in the present, I was in control. It was now my choice to see Dr. Norm. I was an adult, and Dr. Norm would not "just drop me."

I made lists of things that signified independent decision-making. Through journaling, I explored possible reasons for making certain decisions, and questioned what those reasons said about me. I also listed all the differences between the past and the present that related to my decision-making process. Through these exercises, I learned that being "healthy" in the present did not equate to being alone or abandoned.

As Dr. Jim explained, people are not dependent or independent—it's *not* "all or nothing." We are all *inter*dependent.

Finally accepting that I was getting better—and not panicking about it—only came after much repetition of these cognitive strategies.

Exploring issues of control and learning about making my own choices helped me with my feelings regarding Dr. Norm. But I had more work to do.

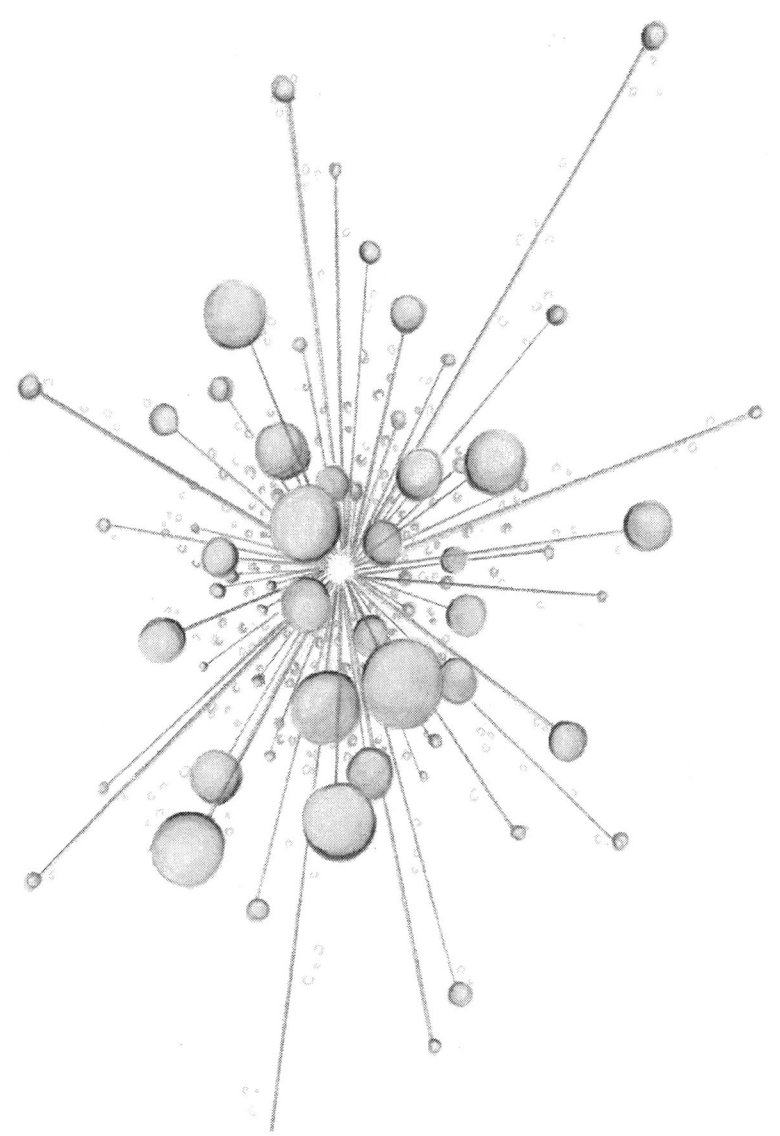

Feelings - after the ice was gone.

I had to learn to accept that I was no longer in danger of being abused if I got better. Dr. Jim reminded me about the "cost-benefit" approach I'd learned about before.

What were the benefits of getting better? What were the costs associated with getting better? Were there any disadvantages to being healthy?

I had to do a lot of soul-searching to answer those questions, since I was in and out of the hospital, constantly in therapy, and I didn't have much experience with being healthy. So how was I supposed to know what the pros and cons were?

Through the charting process, I realized I was afraid of getting better because being healthy meant I would be just another normal person. No longer special. No longer unique.

Equally as strong as the childhood connection I'd made between being sick and being safe at Children's Hospital was the association that being special meant being cared for.

I was only safe from Mother when I was Dad's "Little Dolly." Being "Little Dolly" was special, and "Little Dolly" was safe, protected, cared for by Dad.

If, in the present, I became just another healthy, normal person, I was afraid that meant I wouldn't be special. I'd just be part of the crowd, and I would simply melt into oblivion and no one would care about me.

I didn't understand that each person in the world is inherently special, ineffably unique. How could I? This whole time, I was stuck believing that I was inherently *bad*.

Furthermore, my actress persona had left me with no real experiences interacting with people outside of my childhood family, my present-day doctors and some of the hospital staff. Knowing most people only superficially, I had never come to see how truly individual and unique we all are.

Dr. Jim instructed me to write out lists of people I knew—including my son, my husband, some of the hospital staff who had helped me—and what I thought was special about each of them.

He then asked, "Did any of them have to be sick to be special?"

No. I was beginning to understand.

"Did any of them have to be special in order to be safe?"

No.

These assignments helped me break the connection I had made in my mind that if a person is not special, he or she is vulnerable to being hurt. I now saw how it was possible to be normal and special at the same time.

I started to wonder, does that mean getting better is okay?

Dr. Jim and I then did some work on what I thought I'd be like, as a person, if I was healthy and normal. He had me make a list of qualities I saw in myself that were not connected to my self-concept of being "sick."

For example, I do good artwork, paintings and drawings. I think I'm a good mother and a good nurse. And I believe people should be treated with respect.

Then we went through the cognitive process again.

If I think I do good artwork, what does that say?

It says other people have told me I'm good at art.

And if they said this, then what does that say about me?

It says I have a unique gift that others like.

And what does that say about me?

And we went through this question series with each of the qualities I had listed. The end result was that I finally understood that even if I got healthy I wouldn't fade into oblivion because I *do* have unique qualities and I *am* special to others. I'm a special mom, a special nurse, a special artist.

I learned that I didn't need my dad to call me his "Little Dolly" anymore, and giving that up would not result in getting hurt. I also learned that "getting better" would not detract from my value as a person. Amazingly, I finally learned that I didn't need to fear getting healthy, and I didn't need to panic.

I explained all of this during my next session with Dr. Norm. I discussed my treatment with him and he assured me he would not drop me, and that the choice to continue seeing him was *mine*.

The next morning, I did not have a panic attack. The concept of interdependence, and what that says about me, helped me accept—and not fear—the ways my life was improving.

But there were still triggers at home. Even the slightest argument with my husband, or sign of irritation, would send me into a tailspin. Whenever I perceived the slightest hint of anger from him, I knew I was *bad* and all my mother's old messages would kick in.

I would run and hide in the bedroom, or run out of the house, just as I had run away from home when I was a child. Or I would think about getting razor blades to cut myself again. I had to punish myself in some way for being bad.

There was just no way I could accept that maybe Mark simply had a bad day at work and it wasn't my fault. I was sure I was to blame. How many times did I call Dr. Jim in a suicidal crisis because my husband was angry? It didn't matter how insignificant the situation was. And, heaven forbid, if he actually *was* angry about something I did or didn't do! It would be years before I'd be able to not automatically personalize someone else's bad mood.

Yet, even with these setbacks, there was no stopping the progress I was making. My mother's messages were starting to erode away slowly, ever so slowly.

And new feelings, good ones, were emerging.

I found I was no longer content with just doing therapy and watching old reruns on TV.

But—go back to work?

I was more than a little apprehensive: the flashbacks, the panic, everything that happened before I went on disability—would this continue to haunt me in the workplace? Would I be able to handle a new job? I had reservations about diving right back into the environment of a busy medical center.

As luck would have it, a nearby group home was looking for volunteers.

I called Dr. Jim. Would he think it was okay for me to try something new?

He was all for it.

I wrote down the phone number, hemmed and hawed for a few days, and then made the call. I was told I could volunteer as much or as little as I liked, even just one day per week. I jumped at the chance. Although I was anxious, as I had not done anything but therapy for a solid two years, I was also excited. I knew it was time to add something more to my life.

But I was terrified. How do I talk to people? How do I even know where to put my coat? What if I have to go to the bathroom? What if I get lost? A million worries.

This would be my first experience out in "the real world" since giving up my actress persona. I was no longer used to observing real people and imitating their actions to appear "normal." I was no longer a "robot." Could I make it in the world as a real person, with real feelings? Would people accept me?

I volunteered every Wednesday, but I had to work hard to control my fear. I was sure everyone working there could read the glaring signs tatooed on my forehead: "I am a survivor," and "I am a psychiatric patient."

My life revolved around therapy, hospitals, restraints and medication, and I was certain everyone would find out. I was so busy worrying about all of this that I hardly ever spoke. I was very quiet and kept to myself. I ate lunch by myself. Sure, I answered when spoken to, but I never initiated a conversation. It was just too scary.

But I was a hard worker, and the staff saw that. After only six months of volunteering, they offered me a job—as a nurse, no less.

Accepting would mean losing my disability benefits. I discussed my options with my husband, Dr. Jim and Dr. Norm before eventually deciding to take the job. I worked there for the next 10 years.

Although I loved the job, I still had a hard time interacting with my co-workers. It would be years before I could initiate a conversation.

The self-concept my mother had bestowed upon me continued to persist, and I still couldn't bring myself to amend the "No Friends" clause in the Constitution.

Ghosts from the Past

After several years of working there, keeping to myself, one of my co-workers started talking to me. Before I knew how it happened, we started going to the health club together after work.

We worked out together for several months, until *I panicked!* I knew I shouldn't have friends—it was against the law.

And so, I repeated my old pattern of sabotage. Intermittently at first, I told her I couldn't go to the gym because I wasn't feeling well—I had an upset stomach, or some other excuse. Then I started giving her the cold shoulder whenever we passed each other in the hallway. I refused to speak to her. Through my actions and facial expressions, I gave her the impression that I was very angry with her. And although she didn't understand why, she soon got the message, and the "friendship" was over. Finally, I was safe again.

I CONTINUED DOING MY ART, my drawings and paintings, which was ever so slowly cultivating a feeling of self-confidence.

After awhile, I even began to share my art. I started selling some of my paintings at craft fairs. Soon, requests for paintings were pouring in. I couldn't believe it, but people liked my work. For the first time in my life, I felt proud of something I made. My mother was not there to tear up my drawings like she did when I was a child. And I came to believe I actually had something good to offer the world.

My next breakthrough in feeling good caught me by surprise. After I had been working for a few years, I needed to get a second job for financial reasons. My son was now in college, so we had tuition to pay on top of a mortgage and medical bills—prescription bills, therapy bills and hospital bills.

I returned to hospital nursing. Although I was apprehensive, Dr. Jim and I spent several sessions "role playing" my job in the hospital. I was expecting the flashbacks I'd experienced prior to going on disability. I was anticipating I'd have to be my usual stone statue.

Not long after starting at the hospital, I was assigned an elderly patient with heart failure. He and I began talking as I performed the routine medical exams.

He told me all about his family and how he missed his children. And, suddenly, I felt a connection with him. I *felt* for him.

Although I didn't know the word for it at the time, I was feeling compassion.

As we talked, I cried with him. We were two human beings who connected on a very deep, emotional level. I came out from behind my stone wall to give him support.

I had now found joy, not only in my art, but also in being a nurse. The remarkable thing was that I was truly present in that moment, not only enough to feel for my patient, to cry with him, but present enough to notice that this moment of empathy would not have been possible without all my years in therapy. I *was* changing.

I didn't feel comfortable coming out from behind my wall every day, as there were still ghosts from the past lurking out there. But if and when I decided to peek my head out, if only for a glimpse of the outside world, this experience showed me that there were good feelings waiting out there for me, too.

* * * * * *

AROUND THIS TIME I STARTED developing chest pains, but the doctors were unable to determine a cause. My primary medical doctor did an EKG and an echocardiogram, but found nothing abnormal. She ruled out asthma as the cause.

I was frightened, especially since my dad had died of a heart attack. My brother had a history of chest pain as well.

My primary doctor sent me to a cardiologist, who followed me for quite a while, doing further diagnostic tests. One stress echo *did* come back abnormal and I was immediately scheduled for an angiogram. When that came out normal, the cardiologist then told me that the chest pain was most likely a side effect of my psychiatric medication. He said the Tenex I was taking was "messing up my autonomic nervous system."

Finally, I thought, I had an answer. I discussed this with Dr. Norm, and naturally he wanted to talk to the cardiologist. But when I asked him to discuss it with Dr. Norm, he said, "No, I never said that and I'm *not* talking to a psychiatrist!"

That threw me for a loop. How, or why, would I ever make up a reason for my chest pain? Where would I even get such an idea?

He was calling me a liar! I was thrown back into the past, to memories of the police, the priests, and the doctors at the state hospital who never believed anything I told them about what was going on at home.

I couldn't go to work—mentally, I was a 13-year-old child. I was someone who "made things up."

It took weeks to pull me back out of the flashback.

Dr. Jim and Dr. Norm were very supportive, and I made it through this prolonged flashback *without* being hospitalized. I was able to contract for safety.

In the end, I realized I had done nothing wrong, and I got referrals for a new cardiologist who I felt I could trust.

The lesson I learned from all of this? Stand up for what you believe in.

Dr. Norm did change my medication, taking me off Tenex and instead prescribing Clonidine, which ultimately cured the chest pain, but it was not an easy adjustment.

I started taking the new drug during those turbulent weeks when I was consumed by the prolonged flashback. Dr. Norm wanted to gradually wean me off the Tenex while, concurrently, starting me on a low dose of Clonidine.

Within two days of taking both prescriptions, I totally freaked out. I remember going for one of my usual walks around the park—this always helped me relax—and being overcome by the strangest feeling that I was "in a movie."

Nothing felt real. I sat down on a park bench to try to get reoriented, but the sensation only got worse. I saw people walking by, walking their dogs, I saw the trees in the park, but I felt detached from everything. Either I wasn't real, or nobody around me was real. It was a frightening sensation.

I walked home as quickly as I could and called Dr. Norm. His nurse, Dee, answered. I told her I needed to talk to the doctor right away.

I knew Dee could hear the panic in my voice because she stayed with me on the line until Dr. Norm had wrapped up with another patient and took my call.

When Dr. Norm came on, I explained the feeling I'd had in the park, which he understood completely. He called it depersonalization, and immediately had me stop taking Clonidine.

We decided to hold off on any medication changes until I was over the prolonged flashback and more stabilized.

That took about a month. I was then able to stop taking Tenex and gradually starting on Clonidine. The chest pains never returned.

After awhile, I even got to a point where I didn't need to take Clonidine daily, but only during particularly bad episodes of dissociation.

OVER THE NEXT SEVERAL YEARS, although there were still intermittent crises, things were relatively stable. I worked seven days a week, was seeing Dr. Jim once a week after work, and Dr. Norm once a month. I still attended the cognitive therapy group with Dr. Alan on Tuesday nights.

Intermittently, I tried to make friends, but even that would end in tragedy at times.

I began to feel comfortable talking to one of my co-workers. One day we got together when my husband was out of town, and I even told her that I had run away from home when I was little.

That was the first time I had shared *anything* about my past with *anyone* besides my doctors. Sure it was scary, but it felt good in a way, too.

The very next day, she became severely ill and ended up in the emergency room.

No amount of reassurance from Dr. Jim or Dr. Norm could convince me this wasn't my fault. I *knew* she was sick because I had talked to her.

"I *am* the cause of all bad things that happen in the world!"

It all came flooding back to me:
Wasn't having sex with Dad my fault because I couldn't behave?
Didn't I have to urinate outside like an animal because I was bad?
Didn't Paul die when he was five because I killed him?
Didn't our neighbors' house burn down because I didn't behave?
Didn't I need to be locked in the garage for talking to a friend?
Didn't my mother have heart problems and eye problems because I was bad?
Wasn't our house infested with flies because I was garbage?
Didn't people die in the Oklahoma City Bombing because I had an abortion?
Didn't that car crash at the bank happen because I wrote in my journal that I was angry at my mother?
And now, wasn't my co-worker sick because I told her my secrets?
And the list went on. Even though I had already talked about all these things at length with Dr. Jim, this most recent event caused me to go into a psychotic state.

Because of how severely this affected me, Dr. Norm had me taking up to 100mg of Zyprexa per day as needed—the usual maximum dose is 20mg.

I was suicidal again.

I phoned Dr. Norm and told him I was going to kill myself. I was planning on going out into the woods and overdosing on my medication.

He called 911 and had the police search the forest preserves near my home.

But I never did make it that far. In fact, I simply passed out because of the high dose of Zyprexa I was on.

At 11 p.m., I awoke to find myself lying on the bedroom floor—seeing the blinking message light on the telephone answering machine. Dr. Norm had called six times and said he had the police out looking for me.

I called him as soon as I woke up and explained what had happened. He called the police and, within minutes, they were at my door to make sure I was okay.

To this day, I don't know why Dr. Norm didn't hospitalize me.

It took weeks of intense therapy to get me out of that psychotic state, out of the flashback, and I had to take some time off work. The problem was, and continued to be, magical thinking. It was so hard to believe that my mother wasn't sending me messages about "misbehaving" and "telling secrets."

Logically, I knew there weren't any "Little People" following me around. But on an emotional level, every trigger still made me feel like that same bad little girl.

With a lot of cognitive therapy, I was finally able to return to work, but that still hadn't changed my magical thinking.

※ ※ ※ ※ ※ ※

In 1999, my mother died.

I survived without being hospitalized.

Mother was diagnosed with metastatic cancer, and suffered for months before passing away. I had neither seen nor spoken to her in quite some time—not since our confrontation in the restaurant several years before.

When I was told she had cancer, I immediately felt guilty. Both of my parents had always told me that my mother's medical problems were my fault—so, naturally, this was no different.

I blamed myself for ever talking to Dr. Jim and Dr. Norm about "family secrets." I knew doing so was a violation of all Mother's rules, and I wasn't sure what my punishment should be.

In any case, I knew the least I could do was to go see her again. She was under hospice care for months, and I went to see her almost every day.

Our relationship was strained, to say the least, but I felt this was something I *had* to do. Surprisingly, I didn't panic during these visits, but her death did throw me.

She had always told me that you have more power in death than in life.

And, now, I believed that since she was dead, she could and would come after me to punish me in some way.

Once again, my doctors and I used cognitive therapy to dispel the magical thinking, and we used the art therapy techniques I had learned in the hospital.

I made many collages and drawings and eventually regained a feeling of safety. I had survived another crisis.

Magical thinking was something I've had to contend with my entire life.

As Dr. Jim explained to me, magical thinking is normal in young children. They believe they are the center of the universe, that everything revolves around them, and they cause things in their world to happen. But, as we grow up, we develop a more realistic perspective on the cause-and-effect relationships at play in the world.

I, on the other hand, was never able to dispel this magical thinking because it was constantly reinforced by my parents. They repeatedly told me that I caused things, bad things, to happen. They did this, according to Dr. Jim, as a means of controlling me, first through fear and then through punishment.

How could I have caused a house to burn down simply by "not behaving right" if it weren't for magic? How could I have caused my mother's medical problems, if not by magic? How could lighting or refusing to light a candle cause bad things to happen, if magic didn't exist?

The list from childhood goes on and on. I was taught to believe in magic.

Since I believed (had no choice but to believe) what my parents told me, I always knew that if something bad happened either to me, someone I cared about, or even to people I didn't know, I was the cause of it.

It's a very hard thing to release the spell of magical thinking—I could always come up with what I thought was a reasonable explanation for every incident I blamed myself for. I could relate every catastrophe to something I did wrong. A co-worker became ill when I talked to her. The Oklahoma City Bombing occurred when I had an abortion. A car crash happened when I wrote about my mother in my journal.

The list from adulthood goes on and on. I still believed in magic, unquestioningly.

Changing this thought process was a daunting task. How can you disprove the existence of magic?

Dr. Jim and I spent many sessions debating the magical power I believed I had.

But he was persistent; he was logical. The first step in changing anything is an understanding of where it came from. He proposed that my parents told me these things not because they were true, but to control me through fear. There were several logical, "non-magical" reasons that explained my parents' behavior.

As a child, I was a rebel. I tried to stay away from my mother and not go anywhere with her. I was sleeping with my father and telling a lot of people about it, about being beaten, about the bathtub rituals and how my mother had abused me with her dental instruments.

No amount of beatings ever deterred me from talking, but my parents did not want their secrets discovered. So, they resorted to mind control. Simple punishments—beatings or even locking me in the garage or the crawlspace did nothing to make me listen. I still slept with dad, and still continued to try talking to the police, the priests, anyone I could find.

Dr. Jim and I had many discussions about what motivated my parents to lie to me about being bad, why they told me that I caused bad things to happen when, in fact, I didn't—when, in fact, that was not possible because magic doesn't exist.

As I began to slowly understand their motivation, I began to question the validity of their messages. Then, for the first time in my life, I began to question the existence of magic.

Dr. Jim gave me homework assignments based on cognitive therapeutic techniques. In my journal, in one column, I listed the bad things I thought I caused. In the second column, I listed what I had done wrong to have caused each of these. I included examples from both my childhood and adulthood.

Then came the hard part. In the third column I had to list possible alternative explanations for the events. For example, I wrote Timothy McVeigh next to the Oklahoma City Bombing.

I wrote that there could have been an electrical fire, or a gas leak in my neighbor's house that had caused the fire. I wrote that in my mother's family there was a history of heart problems. I wrote that the car crash I believed I had caused was actually the result of an elderly driver simply stepping on the gas instead of the brake.

Dr. Jim and I discussed how I felt about each of the alternatives in the third column. It was scary. Accepting that I really didn't cause these things would mean giving up an ideology I'd clung to my entire life.

For the very first time, I found myself considering the possibility that sometimes bad things happen, and it's just a part of life.

That was really hard to accept. It was a lot easier thinking I was in control. That was true for me as a child and as an adult.

As a child, although I was really scared when my mother told me these things, in some way, it gave me a sense of power, of control, in an otherwise chaotic childhood.

As an adult, this world view continued to give me an even greater sense of control—at least I knew when to punish myself. I didn't have to wait for my mother to do it, or for the "Little People" to find me.

Dr. Jim was very patient and supportive as I discovered these alternative explanations and my reasons for holding onto them.

He understood how hard it was to give something up without replacing it with something else. The ultimate goal was to give up the underlying belief that I was bad, but he knew I wasn't ready for that yet. So, for now, we focused on giving up magical thinking. And since having control was a key point, we discussed the concept of "personal power."

We explored what a person actually does have control over. For example, I have control over my actions and how I treat other people. I have control over whether my actions are consistent with my values. This part was easier for me to understand—I knew how important it was to treat others well, to treat them with respect. I knew how important it was for a child to be loved. That's how I'd raised my son. Slowly, I came to realize there are *good* things I had control over. Realizing that did give me a sense of "personal power," as Dr. Jim put it.

This took many sessions with Dr. Jim, a lot of journaling, a lot of cognitive therapy, and a lot of patience—not only from Dr. Jim, but also from myself.

At long last, I began to conceive of a world with no magic.

Magical thinking still came up as an "automatic thought" from time to time. But each time it happened, I learned to break the cycle faster and faster by remembering my list of alternative explanations.

My periods of crises started becoming shorter and shorter, as I grew stronger.

I still needed time off from work occasionally, but noticing that there was no world tragedy that followed my mother's death gave me courage.

And my asthma had gone into almost complete remission by this time. I had gone from constant asthmatic symptoms to a minor flare-up only once or twice a year.

My medical doctors were amazed at the improvement. Dr. Jim expected it.

Dealing with Halloween every year was still a problem, even though I had integrated all of the alters, including "She," who had blamed herself for Paul's death.

Still, I was plagued by guilt every Halloween. I still hadn't totally forgiven myself for my friend's death.

Although, as I said before, I will never be sure if Paul really died that night, or if it was merely staged as a means of controlling me, I was still haunted by the flashbacks and riddled with guilt.

Dr. Jim and Dr. Norm told me over and over again, "No matter what really happened, a five-year-old little girl is *not* responsible for someone's death."

It didn't help that at work, they decorated for Halloween and covered all the windows with aluminum foil, and turned the entire place into a haunted house.

For several years, I called in sick on Halloween. I could *not* get Paul out of my mind until 2007.

* * * * * *

It was 2006, and I was becoming more and more skilled at weathering crises without needing to be hospitalized. On some days I still felt the need to be an actress, but I was learning that fighting feelings didn't help.

It would take years of practice before I'd be able to fully accept, tolerate and "sit with" all my feelings. In the meantime, Dr. Jim and I developed some techniques and imagery to help me keep my emotions from controlling me.

I would talk to myself—to calm myself. I would imagine that a feeling was just a boxcar and visualize the train chugging along down the track without stopping. Along the same theme, I also imagined a memory as leaf floating down a swiftly-moving river. And there was always the thought vacuum and my mental safe, where I could lock a feeling away if I needed to take a break.

When I'd get scared or angry, Dr. Jim said, "Try to not give it energy. Don't focus on it. Giving it mental energy will only make it stronger."

Dr. Jim taught me that there were distinctions between what I thought were similar emotions. For example, I had to learn to differentiate between anger and rage, between anxiety and panic, between sadness and grief, between choice, responsibility and blame.

The distinctions and degrees of various emotions were blurred to me since I had learned at an early age that even a minor problem would escalate into a catastrophe with frightening results when my mother started raging or beating me.

So Dr. Jim suggested I make two "scales." I made a "Catastrophe Rating Scale," and a "Running Rating Scale." I listed various things that had gotten me upset, as well as future possibilities of events that had the potential of upsetting me.

Then I had to think, realistically, "Exactly how dangerous *is* the event—and is it truly worth running away from and getting suicidal over?"

I saw, after putting this all in writing on a poster, that a flashback is *not* truly dangerous in the present. It poses no physical threat.

Also, I learned that feeling "I'm bad" is not a catastrophe to run from or kill myself over ... it's just a thought.

In the end, there weren't many things on the list that could actually be categorized as catastrophes—except maybe a damaging tornado or a major heart attack. Through this assignment, I was learning to give up running. I kept this poster handy at home, so I could refer to it whenever the impulse to run started to overwhelm me.

I learned that if I allowed myself to feel, to remember without fighting, with support, and by talking about things and by journaling, *this, too, shall pass*.

As Dr. Norm had told me so many years before in the hospital, the memories were now becoming like "pictures on the wall." After looking at them, I could simply walk on by. Another lesson learned.

I was gaining more and more coping skills, and it had now been over eight years since my last hospitalization. I was no longer attending any type of group therapy. I saw Dr. Norm once a month, and Dr. Jim once every other week.

It was time to tackle the fundamental issue: my underlying belief that I was inherently *bad*. I had worked through the actual memories—now it was time to tackle the *belief*. And although I knew it came from my mother, I felt as though it was *part* of me, that it was *inside* me, it was *who I was*. Try as I might, I just couldn't deny who I was.

Dr. Norm's nurse, Dee was instrumental in helping me recover from this belief.

When I first started seeing Dr. Norm as an outpatient, his office was in the hospital. I would call his secretary (whom I never met) to schedule my appointments. When the hospital closed, Dr. Norm moved out to the suburbs and Dee was his new office manager. Over the years, she has become a friend, a confidante to me. How many times did I call the office when I was in a crisis?

Dee would talk to me until Dr. Norm could call me back.

Dee has sent me cards in the mail. She would write in the cards how she knew I was a wonderful person. She always tried, verbally and in writing, to counter my mother's messages that I was *bad*.

Our relationship was rocky at first. As usual, I was scared of getting close to someone, and there were times when I'd go to my appointment, avert my eyes, and avoid talking to her.

I was trying to sabotage our relationship. Dee didn't let me. She was patient.

She didn't pressure me in any way. She waited until I was able to come around; she never gave up on me.

Recently, after I started sharing my artwork, I did a special oil painting, a landscape, for her, as well as some other oil paintings for Dr. Norm.

Dee's painting hangs over her desk in the office.

It really meant a lot to me that she never let me succeed at sabotaging our friendship. She helped me learn that even though I saw myself as *bad*, not everyone else did.

Part Six
MEETING JESSIE

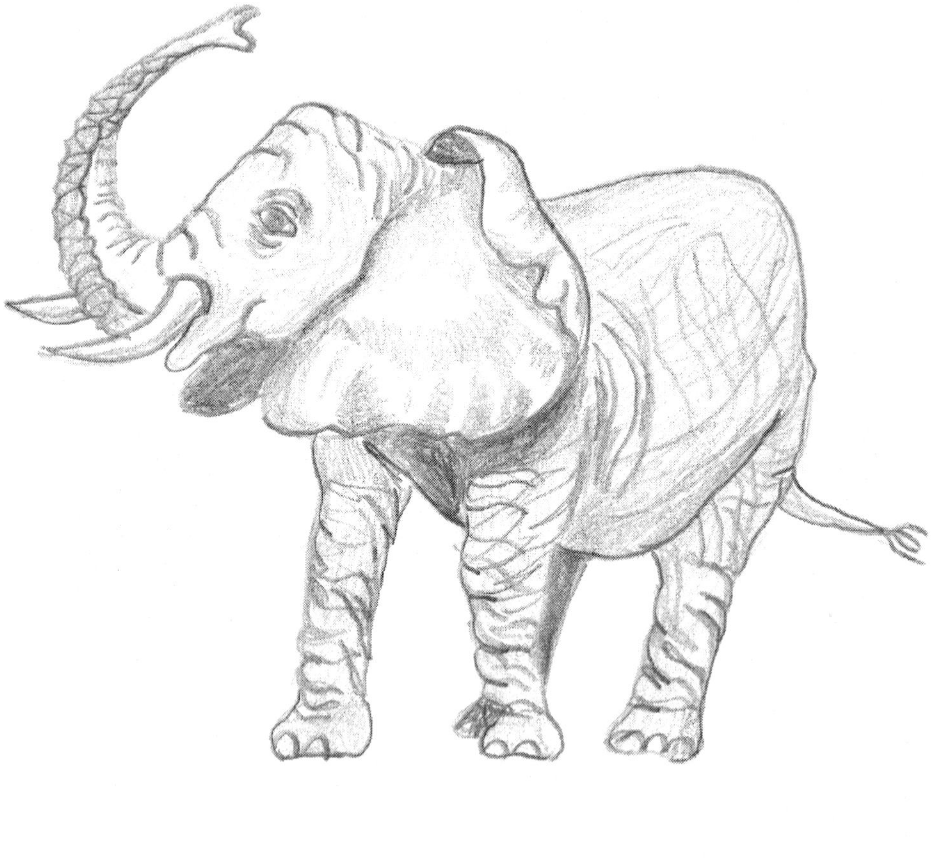

Why, Mommy, Why?

PROPOSED AMENDMENT VIII — 2008 — 49 YEARS OLD

The following amended rules of survival have been proposed. They will be experimented with and then voted upon following a trial period, after which Amendment VIII will be accepted or rejected.

We conditionally amend our decision to never have feelings, based on our ability to tolerate feelings at any given time. We will allow ourselves to have feelings only up to the point of not being overwhelmed. Should any feelings, whether good or bad, start to become overwhelming or intolerable, we can use the following strategies to regain a feeling of safety:

We can draw animals, apples, still life, etc.

We can listen to music on CDs.

We can take a walk.

We can paint a landscape.

We conditionally amend our decision to never have friends. We will allow ourselves to only be as close to a friend as we feel comfortable, and should this begin to feel threatening, whether we get scared, or the friend actually does something hurtful, we will allow ourselves the following strategies to regain a feeling of safety:

We can withdraw for a period of time, for as long as we need to.

We can hold teddy bears at home.

We can confront the person about the hurtful incident.

We conditionally amend our decision to never talk honestly with people. We will use the following strategies to balance honesty with safety:

We will assess each individual person we are talking to, in order to determine if we think they are safe.

We will decide in advance what we think that person is capable of hearing or understanding.

We will not prematurely divulge graphic details of past abuse to friends, as people probably are not capable of hearing this.

We will utilize our doctors when we need to talk about the past.

If we appear to be in danger of being hurt from being honest with someone, it's okay to withdraw for a set period of time.

We amend our decision to always punish ourselves for being social, with the stipulation that since being social is new, and can be overwhelming, we can take pre-planned breaks and spend some private time by ourselves to regain a feeling of safety.

We amend our decision to use cutting ourselves or any other self-abusive behaviors as a first defense.

The following strategies will be used for safety:

Call our doctors

Take PRN medication

Draw some animals/elephants

Hold teddy bears

Take a shower or bubble bath

Listen to music on CD's

Remind myself I am in the present, not the past. Re-state a "Safety Contract" with either of our doctors.

The task of confronting, once and for all, my fundamental belief that *I am bad* set a chain of events into motion that would change my life. Dr. Jim and I set out by discussing what differentiates a good person from a bad person. Is it their actions? Their behavior? Is it inherent? Are we either born one way or the other?

But I found myself stubbornly resistant to moving forward. Or, should I say, my mother's messages were stubbornly resisting our attempts to overwrite them.

Although I agreed with Dr. Jim that no infant is born inherently bad, I could not concede that this was true about myself. No infant is born inherently bad—except me. I'm special. I'm unique. I'm bad.

I became more and more insistent that I was, in fact, a bad person. And I told him I could prove it.

I didn't know what I meant by that. I only knew that I was becoming more anxious by the day. We concluded that it might not be a bad idea to take some time off so I could address this issue more intensely.

At work, circumstances were changing. It had been 10 years since I'd gone off disability, and I'd kept the same job at the group home the entire time. But now questions about continued funding were being raised. Things were getting tense. Relationships were becoming strained. I had been contemplating leaving for a while.

When Dr. Jim and I agreed I could use some time off to devote to therapy, it was the right time to quit.

I did not go back on disability. I had made tremendous progress over the past decade, and I knew I was capable of holding down a job. I had every intention of returning to work before too long. Luckily, at this time, RNs were in short supply.

Dr. Jim and I worked diligently over the summer, and made some progress, albeit without reaching any significant milestones.

A completely unexpected breakthrough came, at long last, only *after* I returned to work in the fall.

I took a job as a hospice nurse, which meant making housecalls as well as seeing patients at nursing homes.

From my very first day on the job, I felt something was wrong.

That first day, I found myself crying inconsolably in the parking lot of a nursing home. I had no idea why I was crying, but I kept crying. After a few weeks, I began hearing a small child crying in my head.

Who was that? I thought I had integrated all the alters years ago.

Was it possible there were more? I shuddered at the thought of more memories, more trauma, more abuse….

No. This was different.

Dr. Jim and I explored why the little girl was crying.

She didn't cry when I'd visit patients at their own homes, only at nursing homes.

It took about a month, before she told us her name. This was Jessie.

We learned she was crying for all those people in the nursing home who didn't have a loving family, no one to care for them.

Jessie said everyone deserved to have a loving family.

As I got to know Jessie better, she started showing me images in my head.

Those were the most disturbing memories of all. Abuse, I could accept. I was used to it. What Jessie showed me was a picture of my mother smiling.

I couldn't accept it. I hated my mother. My mother was angry *all the time*. She hated me, beat me and yelled at me. *My* mother would *never* smile.

But Jessie kept showing me that Mother did smile. She even looked happy.

Jessie said, "I love Mommy."

What!?

There was a part of me that loved my mother!?

I totally freaked out! That was it!

There could be *no part* of me that loved my mother. I would *not* accept that

THE CHANGE

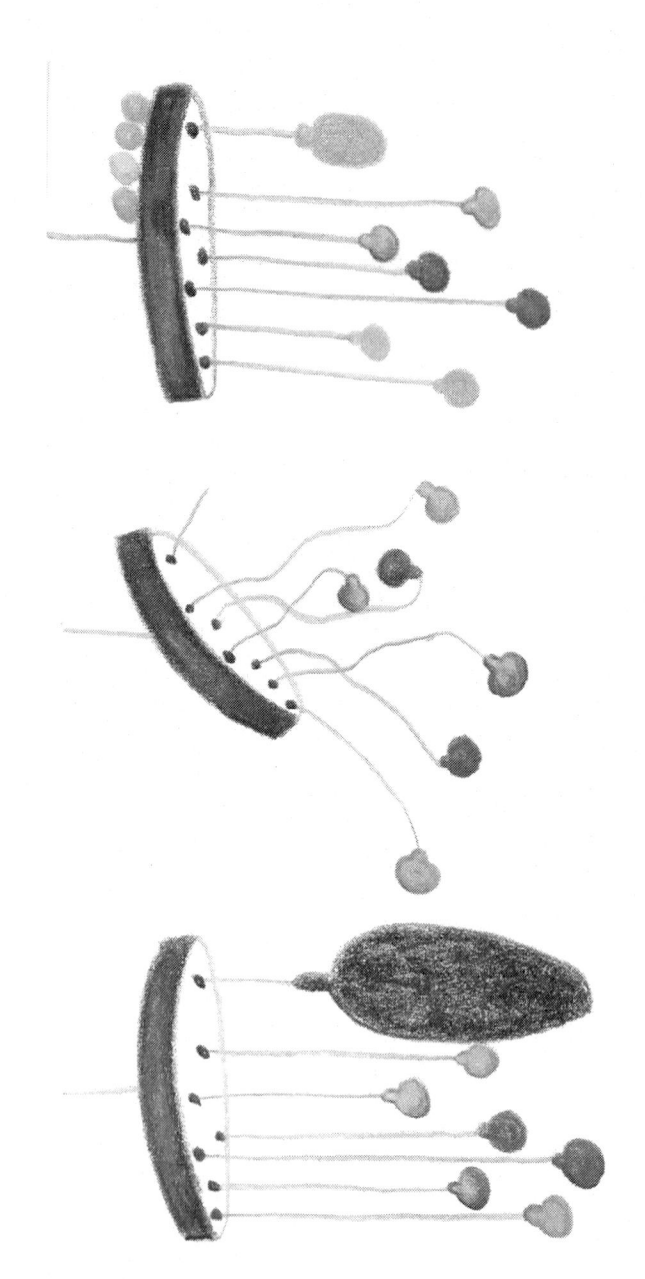

there was any part of me that felt anything but hatred towards her.

"*I hate my mother!*" I screamed.

I don't know if I was trying to convince Dr. Jim, Jessie, or myself.

Dr. Jim said, patiently, "That's okay."

He reminded me of all the lessons I'd already learned.

Running doesn't help. Fighting it makes it worse.

So, together, Dr. Jim and I explored Jessie's memories.

She didn't have many—only a few fleeting instances of my mother actually doing something nice. One time, mom took Jessie to the zoo. Another time she made Jessie a birthday cake.

Even those rare expressions of love were enough to allow Jessie to form a *much needed bond* with her mom. Because of that bond, Jessie felt good about herself. On those rare instances when Jessie was "out" and in control, Mom smiled at her and she smiled back.

Jessie felt loved by her mom. And that's what's needed to begin to love yourself.

Jessie and I had been totally separate for 49 years because I couldn't accept that a good mom could do bad things, or a bad mom could do good things.

I had my view and Jessie had hers. I couldn't reconcile the two. I couldn't accept that I could have loved mom.

Any time I felt love for Mother when I was a child, well, that simply wasn't me. That was Jessie.

I was the bad one—I caused Mom to hate me. Mom and I hated each other. That was the way of the world.

What Jessie represented was unacceptable.

But her memories were undeniable.

I began to *sense* that her memories were true. I knew that what she remembered must have happened. Slowly, I began to accept it.

The hardest part was reconciling the "good mom" with the "bad mom." If I could reconcile the two, what does that say about me?

Does it mean I wasn't really bad after all?

Dr. Jim told me, as he had a hundred times before, "It's not all or nothing. It's not black or white. People have both good and bad qualities."

What helped me most was remembering how I had resolved my issues with dad. I had taken him off his pedestal and eventually came to see him as a human being—with both good and bad qualities.

Could I do this with my mother? My hatred of her was so intense!

Jessie's feelings about Mom were *so* unacceptable they made me panic. I needed to run! I wanted to hide behind being crazy, psychotic.

I needed to test whether or not I could still be crazy. I went to the bookstore and bought a copy of the Satanic Bible and some candles. I wanted to go back to the Mother-and-self concept that I knew so well. I wanted to go back to performing the rituals and believing in evil magic. I wanted to get as far away from what Jessie represented as I could.

I spent two weeks reading the Satanic Bible and lighting candles.

I was frightening myself with what I was doing. I called Dr. Jim in a panic.

He said, "This is not about candles or evil magic. This is about you being afraid of change. You're testing yourself."

He said he was confident I'd pass.

He was right. At my next session, I gave him my copy of the Satanic Bible. His unwavering confidence in me had helped me find the resolve I needed to confront my fear of change. It was time to get back to work with Jessie and stop running.

Jessie felt unconditionally *good* about herself. And, the more we talked, shared, and got to know each other, I began to feel her inner worth.

Locked away for so long, Jessie was the part of me who had been protecting the *good* feelings that were too dangerous for me to have all this time.

A part of me had always known I might want them back again someday.

Through my interactions with Jessie, she has given me love, joy, spontaneity and friendship. She didn't need to be "on guard" with people, to be a "stone statue" or an "actress."

She had saved me for myself.

Yes, somehow, because Jessie had had a "good" relationship with her—*with my*—mother, however brief, it was enough to create a feeling of self-confidence.

Jessie was spared from the messages that I was the *bad* one, that I caused bad things to happen. Jessie was spared the beatings, the abuse, the candles, the messages, spared everything.

The only times she was "out" as a child were for those brief, fleeting moments when mom smiled at her, *at me*.

I wasn't present during those times. I probably couldn't have understood or tolerated the confusion. It probably would have only served to reinforce the idea that being abused really *was* my fault. After all, who could blame a "good" mom?

Separating these experiences was the only way to survive.

Jessie had to remain hidden all these years because she, likewise, wouldn't have been able to accept that her "good mom" could have done all those horrible things.

As Jessie shared her feeling of self-worth, it was giving me the confidence to begin to live a new life.

Through Jessie, I finally learned, *"I am not bad."*

Now that I had finally learned to separate the person I was from the person my mother told me I was, I needed a creative way to silence the old messages whenever they started playing again.

To do this, Dr. Jim and I came up with the idea for a board game. I called it, "My Mother's Game."

The squares I could land on included:
Your childhood home. Go back one square.
Your home today. Roll again.
Making a new friend. Move forward three squares.
Sabotaging a friendship. Go back one square.
Listening to the Old Messages. Go back three squares.
Confronting your mother. Take a recovery card.
Feeling guilty about being sexually abused. Take a recovery card.
Recovery Cards included:
A session with Dr. Jim.
Call a friend.
Go for a walk.
Paint a picture.
Hug a teddy bear.

The object of the game was to get to the final square, which said, "You win! You beat your mother at her own game."

To this day, if I ever get caught up in the old messages, I just ask myself, "Do I really want to play my mother's game again?"

When I finally understood that I was not inherently bad, as my mother had taught me, I came to believe that every child is born inherently *good*. I believe that the events around us change our concept of self.

I was inspired to do an oil painting of a sunlit river flowing through a forest with trees lining both sides of its banks. The river flowed away into a blue sky at dawn.

The sunrise over the horizon represents a child's birth. The river flowing through dark trees, but still reflecting the light, represented that a child's inner self remains strong despite any adversity, or even being abused.

I gave this painting to Dr. Jim, and it hangs in his office to this day.

ARMED WITH THE KNOWLEDGE THAT I was not inherently bad, I was able to revisit the issue of Paul's death. I needed to face those ghosts, once and for all.

Dr. Jim and I went back once again to that Halloween night in 1963.

Maybe Paul died, maybe it was staged. All I know is that was the last time I saw Paul. He was gone. His family moved away.

Paul had been a rebel. Whether his death was a charade or not, it was orchestrated to teach me a lesson, to break me of that same quality—to control me, I now knew.

The Memory of Paul

As Dr. Jim and I talked, I started to cry for Paul for the first time in my life.

Up until now, I had only dealt with the facts, the events. I had never *felt* anything except fear.

The curtain of the fear and panic pulled back. Behind it, there were tears. I was finally able to give up my sense of self-blame, guilt, and responsibility.

I now fully realized that, whatever had happened, it was the adults' responsibility —my mother's responsibility—to bear. Not mine.

As understanding emerged and defeated the guilt I'd been carrying with me for 40 years, there was finally room to feel anger and sadness. I was angry at my mother, and I was *so* sad that my little five-year-old friend, Paul, was gone from my life.

For all these years, I'd never able to grieve the loss. Dr. Jim was very supportive during this time of pain. He encouraged me to talk about my feelings, write about them, and do drawings and collages.

Although this was a difficult time for me, never once did I feel suicidal or self-destructive. I knew, somewhere deep in my heart, that I needed to do this: these buried, once unacceptable feelings needed to be aired.

It took several therapy sessions to completely work through all of these emotions, but in the end, I experienced a profound sense of relief, more powerful than anything I had ever felt.

A lead weight was lifted from me, my iron curtain of fear was raised. I had finally gotten to the fundamental issue of how a little girl felt about losing someone special to her.

I wrote a goodbye letter to Paul. At last I could let him go.

The next Halloween, I did not panic, I did not become suicidal. I simply remembered the sadness of losing a friend.

Another lesson learned: allowing myself to feel was the only way to let my feelings go.

I'd never realized how much a prisoner I had been to Paul's death until I was free to truly feel the sadness of losing him.

That realization opened a seemingly bottomless pit of loss. I now saw there were other prisons holding me.

I told Dr. Jim I really didn't want to talk about Dad and Aunt Maureen, but mourning Paul released a whole flood of walled-off emotions I'd never felt at Aunt Maureen's, or at Dad's, funeral.

"I don't want to lose them again!" I said.

Dr. Jim told me that instead of focusing on their loss, to write about or draw pictures of the special times I'd had with both of them. Even though the person may be gone, Dr. Jim said, no one could take away your good memories of them.

I decided to make a "memory book" for each of them. I looked through old photo albums I'd kept all these years and finally found some pictures of me and my dad, and me with Aunt Maureen.

In the memory books, I included the photographs and short descriptions of the good times we'd had. It felt good to go through my memories of them—I had hidden behind my stone wall for so long.

When I shared these books with Dr. Jim, I cried about the losses for the first time in my life.

Admitting I missed them gave me a new realization: people *are* important in a person's life. The depth of pain of losing someone is related to the intensity of good feelings, of love, you felt when they were with you.

It was painful to admit that loss hurts. But the memories, the good feelings, and the books are mine to keep.

Taking this emotional journey now did *not* cause an asthma flare-up, suicidal thoughts, or panic.

I QUIT MY JOB AS a hospice nurse because it was too stressful and, within a short time, I found a new nursing position.

This time, it didn't take me five years to start talking to my co-workers.

Making conversation comes naturally now.

But sometimes I'm still surprised when I catch myself saying, "Hi. Good morning," to people I pass in the hallway.

Jessie had been the part of me who was not scared, and integrating with her dramatically decreased my fear of people, of friends.

I'm not terrified of going to a company Christmas party—and last year, I actually enjoyed myself there.

I started taking the initiative to call friends to go out for dinner. I'm starting to have real friendships. The little things that others don't think twice about are finally becoming a part of my life.

Then, the good feelings that came with having friends triggered another memory.

Although I did have a flashback, it was a minor incident compared to my previous suicidal crises. The self-confidence and self-concept Jessie had given me lent me the strength to deal with whatever came up.

While I truly enjoyed myself while out with my friends, talking over dinner or coffee, afterwards, when I came home, I'd get extremely anxious.

My friends didn't do or say anything to upset me, and there was nothing at home that was scary. This was reminiscent of how I'd felt years before when I came home from my appointments with Dr. Norm. But I'd resolved that. Why was I having this reaction now?

Dr. Jim said, as he always did, "You'll have your answers."

I journaled and drew about my feelings for a week, all the while becoming more and more anxious.

Dr. Jim said I was reacting like a kid, so I knew it was another case of having to separate the past from the present.

And, sure enough, after a few more weeks of writing, drawing and talking things through, I had a flashback.

I was holding a bell. I couldn't get the image out of my mind.

Dr. Jim asked me to describe it.

"It's shiny and silver."

"What else can you remember about it?"

"It's a bicycle bell," I said. Then, suddenly, I remembered exactly what had happened when I was a child.

During the time when I was my dad's "Little Dolly" and I was special to him, Dad would take me with him when he went for his Saturday morning walks to visit his friends.

I treasured those walks with Dad. I felt important. I felt cared for—a far cry from how I felt at home, being *bad* all the time. During these walks, Dad's friends got to know me, and I them. I learned from Dad what having a friend meant. He taught me how friends treat each other.

Although I couldn't use those skills until 2008, since my mother constantly punished me for trying to talk to people, these lessons from dad *were* learned. I locked them away for safe-keeping until I would be able to use them.

Dad's friends treated me wonderfully. One of his best friends owned a hardware store and, one Saturday morning, this man gave me a special gift: a shiny, silver bell to put on my bike.

I was excited! I was ecstatic! And when Dad and I got home, he screwed it onto the handlebars on my bike. I was so happy that I even forgot, for a little while, how *bad* I was.

That only lasted until my mother saw the bell.

She was furious. "How dare a bad girl take a gift! You don't deserve *anything!*"

She unscrewed the bell and smashed it with a hammer, and then out came the leather strap.

She had to beat it into me that I didn't deserve gifts, much less friends.

"Don't you listen to me? I told me over and over, again, you are a bad girl and you are *not* to have friends!"

And, even more than that, mother made it clear that I could *not*, ever, go with Dad on his walks again.

My bell was gone.

My friends were gone.

I learned to associate coming home, after feeling good with friends, with my mother's rage.

I finally had my explanation of why coming home after a dinner out with my friends in the present made me so anxious.

Dr. Jim and I discussed how all of my fear, my anxiety, was again based on a child's belief that she was bad.

I had to break the connection between the past and the present.

I had to "talk to myself"—explain to myself that I had done nothing wrong as a child by simply going for a walk with Dad, and I was doing nothing wrong now by having dinner with my friends.

The "interpretation" of this being bad was just another example of my mother trying to scare me, to control me.

It was easy to understand my fears about friends today now that I understood where that mindset originated.

Through journaling, talking, and drawing about how the idea that *friends equal being bad* only came from my mother, and was not in fact based on any truth, I was finally able to accept that there was no longer any danger. My mother couldn't take these friends away from me, and I didn't have to worry that I was *bad* and didn't deserve friends.

Miraculously, the next time I had dinner with my friends, I was at peace.

I came home and was able to savor the good feelings without having them overshadowed by fear.

Reliving the memory of going with Dad and being punished was exhausting—but it was worth it. Now that I had a frame of reference for understanding my anxiety, it was gone.

Today I look forward to my time out with friends and I feel relaxed afterward.

Mother, and her messages, are gone. I am learning that people need not be feared. I am learning that friendship need not be avoided at all costs. These were old laws of survival set forth in the Constitution that I just didn't need anymore.

I am learning that there is even fun to be had in life!

It has been over two years since my last episode of cutting myself—another Law I no longer need.

At the time, I *needed* to believe my mother's messages in order to survive. I needed to believe that I was indeed bad. Because that afforded me at least some measure of control, thinking, maybe, just maybe, if I behave better, if I act differently, if I just try harder to listen, maybe Mother won't hate me so much, won't beat me so much.

But I am an adult now. I've learned from Dr. Jim that I can make my own choices.

And I have a new "tool box" to use, and I have friends.

It has taken me over a year to fully accept what Jessie represented.

I think one of the reasons she stayed hidden for longer than the other alters is that she held *hope*.

I could not *feel* this hope and survive the abuse at the same time. That would have hurt even more. That would have been intolerable. It would have meant *hoping* it would end and admitting to myself that I wanted—needed—love from my mother.

Even hope would have jeopardized my safety because, as originally set forth in the Constitution, one of the first Laws of Survival was: Stay as far away from Mother as possible.

But with Jessie's help, I've come to accept two basic truths: I am not bad; and every child, including me, wants, needs, and deserves to be loved.

Yes, it still hurts to think of all that has happened to me, but I was and am a Survivor, and I have healed.

I'll never know: *Why, Mommy, why did you do those things to me?*

But I've given up the hatred.

Jessie gave me the freedom to forgive.

I've forgiven Mom, and this has set me free.

I now can say I truly love my husband and son. I have a caring circle of friends. And I have found joy in my art, in walking, in painting, and in my work.

In December of 2008, nine years after her death, I was finally was able to write this letter to my mom.

Dear Mom,

I need to tell you how my feelings have changed.

Do you remember our conversation at the restaurant when I confronted you about some of the things that happened when I was a kid? About you beating me with the leather strap, and about you blaming me for sleeping with dad? I was really angry and was yelling at you at that restaurant.

Well, for all those things you did to me as a kid—they were wrong, they really hurt me, and, yes, I'm angry about those things —

But I've come to a point now where I can say: "I forgive you." For so many years, I went along, day in and day out, hating you for all the abusive things you did to me. And those things really screwed up my life. But, I'm letting go of the hate. I just don't need it, or want it, anymore. I want a second chance at a life that is not consumed by hatred.

After years of therapy, I've come to see both myself and you differently. I can look at you with a different perspective. Now, instead of hating you, it makes me *sad* that you never got a second chance in life—you never got the help you needed so that you could have been happy. All I can think now is how terribly mixed up, miserable, angry, and troubled you must have been inside in order to do the horrible things you were capable of doing to your own daughter, me.

I'll never know what went so wrong in your life to make you so horribly mixed up—but now I truly feel bad for you. It's sad that you couldn't have gotten help.

And so I forgive you. Maybe it's too late now that you're gone. But at least it's not too late for me. For the past 18 years, I've been plagued by depression, asthma, flashbacks, panic, suicidal crises, you name it. But now I'm finally getting to experience a feeling of calm, of peace. I have finally learned that I am not bad, and I do not cause bad things to happen. Yet true peace includes being free of hating you.

What you did to me was wrong. Nothing will ever change that. But by forgiving you, I am freeing myself.

Peace,

Jody

Joy

Why, Mommy, Why?

Conclusion

As I've been writing this book, I've realized that it's hard to believe all the horrible things I've been through—both as a child, and as an adult. What's so hard to believe is the fact that after I started therapy because of my asthma, I went through six years of hell before I felt any good effects on my life in the present. From 1992 to 1998, I was in and out of psychiatric hospitals, restraints and Intensive Care Units, and going in and out of suicidal states. And it wasn't until the last few years, since 2007, that my life has begun to change and I began to appreciate that life is good.

Even after meeting and then integrating the alters, the biggest influence on making my life better in the present was meeting Jessie—who said she had a good mom. I suppose that's true because, as I've stated throughout the book, the memories of abuse and the actual events weren't nearly as hard to deal with as the unlearning *message* I took away from my childhood: *I was bad.*

Jessie helped me see my mother as a human being and that there always was a part of me that wasn't bad. I realized my mother had no evil magic.

When I finally did get to a place of seeing my mother as just a sick human being, with both good qualities and bad, I could give the control, the blame, back to her. I could then accept that I wasn't bad, I wasn't responsible for any of the abuse, or any other problems in the world. I had nothing to do with our neighbor's house burning down; I did not cause the Oklahoma City Bombing; I shouldn't have been beaten for urinating outside like an animal, etc. I did not need to punish myself further. I did not need to kill myself. It was only my mother trying to control me.

I've been grieving the loss of my childhood ever since I recovered my first memories. But now I can grieve that I didn't have a healthy, supportive mom to guide me through life. And the good news is that the sadness of grief is now balanced with the goodness of having true, caring, supportive friends.

Would I go through all this therapy again if I had the choice, knowing the end results? Well, I've been through hell and back. But on the other hand, I honestly don't think I would have ever dropped the "actress" persona, never would have gotten to experience what real feelings are, what joy is, were it not for therapy. I probably would have gone on sabotaging friendships and being a loner if not for therapy. I would have never gotten to do my art and my oil paintings. And I probably would have died from either suicide or from one of the worst cases of asthma the doctors had ever seen.

Changing the *"I'm bad"* message was the catalyst to a better life. Could I have gotten to a place to do that without going through all the memories—both mine and the alters'? Change comes through understanding, and understanding comes through knowledge. So, *yes*, it was worth it.

But, I still wonder: *Why, Mommy, Why?*

Further amendments to the Constitution can be proposed as the situation warrants.

Why, Mommy, Why?

Easy Recipes

Dr. Jim and I are discussing all that I've learned and reviewing strategies to use should any further problems arise. I have come up with the following "Recipes" for handling potential problems.

A Facing the Problem Recipe

Ingredients:

    1 cup realistic perspective

    ½ cup using a catastrophe rating scale to judge the severity of the problem

    1 tbsp asking: "Just how dangerous is this?"

    1 cup of problem-solving and taking those steps to solve the problem

    May add one—two tsps Ativan as desired, to taste

Glaze:

    1 cup talking to friends

    ½ cup relaxation techniques

Directions:

    Preheat oven to 325. Start with realistic perspective and mix in the rating scale. Add "Just how dangerous is this?" Then add problem solving and those steps. If desired, add Ativan to taste. Grease and flour cake pan, pour batter in pan and cook for two days. Mix talking to friends and relaxation for glaze. When cake is cool, spread glaze and enjoy.

Variations to Add to Basic Recipe

Recipe for confronting a Scary Nightmare/Trigger/Memory
Add to basic recipe:

    1 cup reminding yourself you are an adult

    1 cup separating the past from the present

    2 tsp. Clonidine as desired, to taste

Recipe for solving a Problem with Friends
Add to basic recipe:

    1 cup acknowledging that no one is perfect

    1 cup of trying to work out the problem with them by talking to them

    ½ cup realizing the problem/ hurt may have been unintentional

Recipe for Dealing with a Friend or Loved One's Illness or Problem
Add to basic recipe:

    1 cup empathy

    1 cup recognizing that others' problems have nothing to do with you

    1 ½ cups of helping them with the problem

Recipe for Dealing with a "Catastrophe"
Works best when applied to a car accident, heart attack, tornado and cancer

Add to basic recipe:

    1 cup getting help

    1 cup getting the proper treatment

    1 ½ cups understanding you did nothing bad to cause this

    ½ cup verifying insurance coverage

    1 cup recognizing that adverse events sometimes do occur in life without blaming yourself